THE RED FLAGS I'VE (REPEATEDLY) IGNORED by Brianna McCabe
Published by IG Introspections, an imprint of Inspired Girl Publishing Group
inspiredgirlbooks.com

Inspired Girl Publishing Group is honored to bring forth books with heart and stories that matter. We are proud to offer this book to our readers; the story, the experiences, and the words are the author's alone.

The stories portrayed within *The Red Flags I've (Repeatedly) Ignored* are based on actual events. In some incidents, characteristics, names, and timelines have been changed, compressed, or combined to protect the privacy and preserve the anonymity of people involved. Additionally, certain characters may be composites. The conversations in the book all come from the author's recollections, though they are not written to represent word-for-word transcripts.

This book is written as a source of information only. The information contained in this book should by no means be considered a substitute for the advice of a qualified medical professional. In addition, the publisher and the author assume no responsibility for errors, inaccuracies, omissions, or any other inconsistencies herein. The use of this book implies your acceptance of this disclaimer.

Products, books, trademarks, and trademark names are used throughout this book to describe and inform the reader about various proprietary products that are owned by third parties. No endorsement of the information contained in this book is given by the owners of such products and trademarks, and no endorsement is implied by the inclusion of products, books, or trademarks in this book.

ISBN: 978-1-7373163-7-4
Written by: Brianna McCabe
Editorial & Creative Director: Jenn Tuma-Young
Substantive Editor: Laura B. Ginsberg
Copy Editor: Natalie Papailiou
Front Cover Design: Rodrigo Corral Studio
Book Design and Typeset: Jasmine Hromjak
Photographer: Andy Devaloy
Makeup and Hair Artists: Jonathan Suazo and Bryant Torres
Hair Color Stylist: Jamie Lyn Lane
Library of Congress Control Number: 2022914201

Printed in Bulgaria

THIS BOOK IS DEDICATED
TO ANYONE WHO
HAS EVER DOUBTED
THEIR OWN *self—worth.*

IN *honor* **OF…**

MY MOM, sorry for always stealing swigs of your vodka when I was a broke college kid and diluting the rest of the bottles with water so that the liquid level would remain the same in the hopes that you'd never know. My friends depended on me. I love you. (I promise there's a much cuter and more sincere acknowledgement in the back of this book, but this was way too funny of an opportunity to pass up.)

MY BEST FRIENDS in no particular order (hey mom, blame them), Katie, Aubrey, Joey, Tatianna, Chrissie, Arick, Fran, Jaelyn, Kita, Trever, Haley, Kristen, Chelsea, Justin, Michelle, Mel, and Kelly, thank you for loving me despite (and because of) my antics. My stories wouldn't exist—or at least be half as funny—without each of you. I love you all.

MY MEMA, skip over some of the more R-rated chapters so that I can still be your little, innocent granddaughter in your eyes. I love you.

IN *memory* **OF...**

MY POP, not a day goes by that I'm not thinking of you and your incredibly wholesome presence. I hope that I'm making you proud. I miss and love you.

CONTENTS

PART I
Raunchy Rendezvous

PART II
Roller Coaster Relationships

PART III
Rock Bottom Moments

PART IV
Real Revelations

INTRODUCTION

If you were to ask me to describe myself in a one sentence, I'd probably respond with something along the lines of: I'm your not-so-typical twenty-something-year-old woman with a quirky personality, lionesque-like mane of curls (well, at least until I was introduced to the heat damage of a hair straightener), contagious cackle, and inviting smile who's oddly obsessed with binging Adam Sandler movies, immersing myself in cultures of the world, indulging in cheeses of all sorts, singing (well, butchering) Ginuwine's *Pony* at dive bar karaoke nights, and smelling old books (and fresh cans of tennis balls... which is weird because I don't even play tennis).

As an adjunct professor of public speaking and general communications, you'd think that I'd have an elevator pitch nailed at this point—especially given the fact that it's one of the first assignments with which I task my students. Oddly enough, though, I always just wing my thirty second-long pitch and cater it to the audience I'm speaking to. It's the marketer in me. When I'm not teaching at a university part-time a few nights a week, I'm a full-time marketing professional.

Although my schedule is jam-packed with work, I somehow still managed to tack on the hobby of endlessly chasing after bad boys. (No, not the stereotypical ones that you see in movies, but the ones your favorite meme accounts describe as **red flags.**) Yeah, it was exhausting. While I may jokingly share that I'm not-so-typical in many ways, I have endured the typical (and universally understood) feelings of love, lust, and heartbreak. You know, those swooning and spooning stages that end in aching and breaking. Except for me, it became almost *too* frequent and not-so-typical in its own self-destructive way. Each time

I had thought I had finally found "the one" who I was meant to spend the rest of my life with, an event would trigger me into realizing that the vision I had in my mind of said person didn't *actually* exist and I was instead running into dead-end walls similar to Wile E. Coyote as he smashed into a made-up mural thinking that he finally captured the Road Runner. Like the cartoon, my taste in toxic men was just as loony.

I didn't want to spend my life forever chasing after someone that wasn't meant for me.

And I also don't want you to waste any more time chasing after people that aren't meant for you, either.

To practice what I hope to preach to each and every one of you throughout this book, I had to first understand my overall attraction to these men and dissect the peculiar comfort that I felt in accepting a life of these dysfunctional patterns. The only way that my Type A brain could initially organize all of these thoughts and factors was through writing.

I've always had a passion for writing. After all, I can't just have a crooked *writer (n.)* tattoo on my wrist for no reason (my OCD-like tendencies cringe every single time that I look down). I really refined my love of writing in college when I decided to pursue a bachelor's degree in journalism. I sat in my "Intro to Journalism" class with one of my professors whose background and expertise simply blew me away. My mind a blank paper, I let his lectures leave an imprint like that of the ink of a typewriter. He changed the course of my life during those four years for the better. I enrolled in several of his section offerings, worked my way up to eventually become the editor-in-chief of his student-run newspaper, and together we basked in admiration at this intricate art. He welcomed me back as his graduate assistant when I returned to campus in pursuit of my master's in business administration while working at my full-time job. I didn't realize it at the time, but he essentially became the father that I never had—yet so deeply yearned for.

Okay, so I digressed a little, but yeah, there are some daddy issues that you'll learn about. I guess you could say that growing up without a dad has impacted the way that I view men in general and even relationships as a whole—but the truth is, that's just barely scratching my soul's surface. So like I said, to navigate through all of these experiences I turned to my trusted "happy place" (there's my first Sandler reference of many): my keyboard and a blank Microsoft Word document. At first, it started with poetry. Stanzas eventually started filling 8½ x 11 sheets of canvas. Coffee was copiously consumed in amounts that I'm not necessarily sure would be deemed healthy by any means. Yawns rhythmically scattered throughout the days as I nocturnally typed so as to not lose my thoughts. And thus, the idea for *The Red Flags I've (Repeatedly) Ignored* was born.

By picking up and reading this book, pretty soon you'll know every little thing about me: the wild nights out with friends, the terrible mistakes I've made, the ways I've been downright horrible to my body, the times that I've put up with way too much (hell, some of it was actual abuse), the excessive drinking and partying to mask my innermost pain, the family dynamics… all of it. I'm practically sprawling out naked across these pages—and not just proverbially, I'm actually *going there* in some of the more scandalous sections.

Naturally, many of you may read this introduction and think, *Why the hell is she doing this?*

Well, while I was "word dumping" and talking to my friends about these experiences, I realized that I wasn't alone in my feelings. After all, many people chase after dead-end relationships and deal with red flags, but what's not-so-commonly discussed is the emphasis on the lessons that we learn and the *why* factors that pushed us toward these predicaments:

- *Why* do we ignore these red flags?

- *Why* do we sometimes rationalize the red flags despite seeing them?

- *Why* do we then give our time, energy, and sometimes even physical bodies to said red flags?

- *Why* do we allow ourselves to get hurt over and over and over again?

Don't get me wrong, bookshelves are stocked with relationship reads and general advice-giving guides, but I couldn't quite seem to find a book geared toward women that encapsulated these principles. So, it just made sense to mesh my love of writing with my need to heal—while hopefully inspiring others to do the same.

The Red Flags I've (Repeatedly) Ignored will offer you a deep and rather vulnerable look into my life in the hopes that you can not only understand me at my core, but understand yourself at yours. We're all more than our one-sentence elevator pitches. And though our stories might not be the same, I believe what we all *really* want is: that is, to love and be loved. Deep down inside all of us, there's a person trying to fight past our greatest insecurities and find ourselves within the warm, comforted embrace of not just a romantic lover, but within our own skin as well. Reflecting on my past has shown me that many of my experiences could have potentially been avoided if I had better heeded the red flags and underlying gut instincts that told me to flee the scene. For some reason, though, I felt like my body could take blow after blow like that of a stunt woman. At the time, too, I didn't quite have a story or person to relate to in order to better lead me. That, coupled with a terribly low sense of self-worth, was a nightmare even Freddy Krueger would refrain from.

In full transparency, I'm not proud of some of these stories. You will find me at some of my weakest points that made me question if my moral compass was even still calibrated and pointing north. Anxiety engulfed me at the thought of publishing some of these chapters in fear of potentially losing my jobs, too. What kept me motivated and hushed those fears was knowing that we *all* have stories: some magnificent, some tragic, some embarrassing, some hysterical, and yet they've all been strung together to craft the beautifully empowered characters that each of us is within our own autobiographies.

Whereas some individuals choose to keep their narratives a bit more secretive, others choose to vocalize them—both due to a multitude of motivating factors. For me, my goal is to promote greatness within ourselves and build a self-love even amidst the most fragile of frames. Although it may take some work, we can trust in the fact that there is a profound energy within us. Therefore, this will be a collaborative effort between the two of us through workbook-like tasks.

Right from Chapter 1 we'll begin to identify red flags together so that we can learn to apply these concepts and lessons in real time. For the purposes of my experiences, I'm going to address the red flags as "he" to better align with my stories. However, I encourage you to replace "he" in your head as you read along with the pronoun of your preference. Also, you'll more than likely notice that in some of these chapters I don't point out every single red flag—otherwise, the flow of the stories would be entirely disrupted. Instead, try to find the "hidden" red flags and even scribble some notes in the margins of this book as they pertain to your own life experiences. After all, this is your workbook, too.

We'll also dig deep and reflect together. It has been said that you can't change what you don't acknowledge, so at the end of each of the first three sections I reflect on the root causes of my own distorted decision-making as it pertained to the many (and I mean *many*) red flags. Within these pages, I share how my unhealed traumas infiltrated my life at those very moments and how I now hope to better combat those plaguing experiences to move through life in a healthier manner (and avoid another relationship *Red Flags* book part II). To make more conscious choices moving forward, it's crucial that we go there.

As such, the book has been broken down in the following format:

PART I: RAUNCHY RENDEZVOUS

In this first section, we're sprinting past first base and second base (hell, even third), and going all the way home—and into the sheets—with some of these stories. (To my mom and Mema, please pretend that this section doesn't exist.)

PART II: ROLLER COASTER RELATIONSHIPS

The stories I share in this section show just how much whiplash my heart experienced as it was pushed up and down, back and forth, and even sideways throughout some of my relationships. I thought this was how love was supposed to be: passionate and all over the place.

PART III: ROCK BOTTOM MOMENTS

These are, well, some of the heftier stories that tend to weigh on me like a ball and chain shackled to my heart. I would rather make you laugh at my pain first (Kevin Hart, please don't sue me), and then disclose the deepness.

PART IV: REAL REVELATIONS

Together, we will understand the key takeaways of this book and learn how to avoid red flags and create a better sense of self-worth.

THROUGHOUT THE BOOK

Throughout the book I reveal my unhealthy replacement behaviors of relying on food, sex, and alcohol as temporarily fills as I painstakingly "coped" with my own devastating demons—and this will be a theme that's woven into the following sections as well. While some of you may not relate in those exact manners, I do encourage you while reading to peel back your own layers and pay mind to some of your own unhealthy mechanisms or avoidant behaviors, such as excessive shopping, smoking, gambling, or even running away, as temporary bandages for any open wounds where your self-love has bled—and continues to bleed—out.

At the end of each section there's a "Red Room" for you to really dig in and look intrinsically at yourself, too. I encourage you to grab a notebook and journal your responses to the questions that I pose so that you can begin reflecting on some of your own history. After all, awareness creates understanding so that we can be kinder to ourselves and make choices from a more healed mindset.

By no means is this a man-bashing book or a shot at trying to be a swirling together of E.L. James' *50 Shades of Gray* and Tucker Max's *I Hope They Serve Beer in Hell* with sprinkles of Steve Harvey-like lessons on top like some kind of decadent sundae (though I'm oddly turned on at the thought of that). My intention also isn't to slander the previous men in my life, either. (Trust me when I say that I've done my due diligence in scrubbing my social channels and changing plenty of characteristics to preserve their identities in an effort to allow them to live the most fruitful of lives.)

After all, this book really isn't about *them* at all.

It's about me and you.

What I mean by that is, the partners in our lives should serve as mirrors to reflect back what *we* ourselves are and need to learn. (Hopefully the guys even learned something from me, too.) So let's be clear: I am not a victim; I'm a survivor. (And I can't speak for everyone's circumstances, but I hope that this book helps you become a survivor, too.) I have used these experiences to take accountability, grow, and evolve.

I am both a learner and a teacher (literally). And, as such, through my confessions, introspections, insights, and adventures, if I can help at least *one* "lost" person get back on the road to inner happiness, I will consider that an accomplishment—and, if I can make at least one person laugh, then maybe I'll take this amateur stand-up gig on the road and see if I can be the next Dave Chappelle. (Okay, I'll admit that last one's a stretch.)

⚠ CONTENT WARNING

While some of the stories presented within *The Red Flags I've (Repeatedly) Ignored* may seem exhilarating, alluring, or even entertaining, I do want to stress that several of the situations I've gotten myself into could've been dangerous. In fact, many of my friends have told me that I'm lucky for having avoided what could've been incredibly harmful outcomes with my promiscuous sexual behaviors and alcohol abuse. Please keep this in mind while reading—and know that I'm not condoning any of these behaviors.

To my adolescent and even young adult readers, I would recommend that you close this book and not move forward—unless, of course, your parent or guardian has given you the "go ahead." (I don't want to influence your mind at such an impressionable age with some of the X-rated content contained within the bindings of this book. That's way too much responsibility.)

To my college-aged readers who may be entering new territories of love, lust, and potential pleasuring, make sure that you're safe… unlike how I acted. (Trust me here when I say that yes, you do need to actually listen to your sex education and other general health teachers.)

To my readers who have been through similar situations, I don't want you to feel as if I am suggesting that these fun-sounding antics are encouraged. (I empathize with you entirely.)

To my readers who want to enjoy their sexual liberations and freedoms, I want you to know that it's perfectly okay for you to do just that. (There should absolutely be no victim-blaming and slut-shaming, but there should be conversations and education about consent, boundaries, and what to do in case some form of assault or unsafe practice does occur.) That being said, though, I do encourage living your life to the absolute fullest—just, of course, in a smart and safe manner.

And lastly, I want to reiterate to each and every one of you that you're not alone—and help for whatever you may be going through or dealing with is available. I'm an advocate for mental, physical, emotional, and spiritual health—and I'm proud to share that I wouldn't be where I am today without the help of my therapist, friends, exercise routine, and meditative practices. You, too, may find relief and healing through a therapist, counselor, mentor, support group, or even spiritual guide. Don't be afraid to ask (and seek) for help.

Part One

RAUNCHY

[ˈrôn(t)SHē]

ADJECTIVE

earthy, vulgar, and often
sexually explicit

RENDEZVOUS

[ˈrändəˌvoō, ˈrändāˌvoō]

NOUN

a meeting at an agreed time
and place, typically between
two people

1

THE (Almost) GIRL NEXT DOOR

"Your awkward sexual encounters and dating life are my main sources of entertainment."

Yeah, that's an actual screenshotted text message from my childhood best friend, Lizzy, that I've saved for about seven years now. This was in response to my most recent sexcapade at the time of being vigorously teabagged by a soccer player I knew in college who used my body as his own personal jungle gym as he swung around and grappled me in different areas. Your perspective on life really changes once you make direct eye contact with someone's anus. I pretty much begged for a lightning bolt to somehow strike me dead through his apartment as I laid flat on my back while he sumo squatted over me facing in the opposite direction and continued to speed box my uvula with his third lower leg. (Yes, I'm referring to his giant penis.) I was having a miserable, unrequited experience.

I tend to look back at Lizzy's text from time to time. It initially makes me let out a hearty giggle—then it's quickly followed by an almost natural shaking of my head in disappointment.

"You know you're not going to achieve anything good by allowing men to use you like this, right?" Lizzy later added.

"Stop trying to be a buzzkill!" I typed back.

I still haven't learned.

You see, I was what Lizzy and other friends referred to as a "late bloomer" in that I didn't start exploring my sexuality until later in life when compared to others. I attributed these reservations to my internal battle with my weight, which then translated to this external lack of self-confidence. Selfishly, I wanted to have guys fiending for me, except they seemingly gravitated to women who flaunted their petite frames. So, when I experienced the first nurturing sensations of attention and vitamin D (double entendre) from a man during my seedling stage, I started to slowly sprout—and eventually bloomed and quickly took over several fields as a horny little weed.

I truly went from zero to one hundred when I received my first literal watering by a man (yes, actual spluge to the face, that is) by my around-and-down-the-block neighbor. It all started while I was unpacking my family's belongings from a U-Haul and hoisting boxes into our new home my freshman year of high school when I saw him curiously walk down the street to scope us out. As I wiped the sweat from my eyelids for better visual clarity, I realized that I recognized him from having crossed paths in our high school corridors. It was Seth, a senior on the baseball team who was well over 6 feet tall with flowing dirty blonde hair and an adorable smile. He gave me the most subtle, flirty smirk, ran his fingers through his scalp, and then proceeded on his way down the street.

This entire five-second hypnotic encounter caused me to drop a fairly massive box (and impacted my other box as well, clearly).

"Brianna!" my mom shouted from the back of the truck. *"You have to be more careful!"*

"I know, I know!" I said as I tried to recalibrate from this daze. *"I'm sorry!"*

"Was it one that I marked as fragile?" mom frantically asked.

"Fra-gee-lay," I pretended to slowly read off of the box. *"It must be Italian,"* I added as a reference to *A Christmas Story.*

"Brianna, oh my god!" she said as she jumped out from the back of the truck.

"Mom, I'm just joking!" I laughed. *"Relaaaaax. Wooooosah."*

You know that *feeling* you get as a freshman when you lock eyes with an upperclassman, right? Think about it: I was merely a fish in this vast sea of creatures and you're telling me that a *shark* noticed my pufferfish-of-a-self? (That's a nod to my body dysmorphia.) At this point, I couldn't tell if I was sweating from the exercise of moving or from the excitement of being semi-aroused.

A few weeks later, I received a friend request on Facebook from him followed by a message that said, *"Hey, new kid."* It was at that moment that I also started to simultaneously sweat from my hands. Our conversations weren't anything serious for quite some time. They were fun, flirty, and inquisitive by nature. I think there's always this magnetic draw to your neighbor, especially that (almost but not really) "girl next door" type of fantasy that I think every guy ultimately dreams of.

The messages didn't quite escalate until my junior year of high school. It was at this time that I became a bit more "loose" (no, not my lady parts), but in terms of my partying behavior with my other best friend, Rachel. I'll never forget stories from the first time I got drunk. Well, *alright*, I myself forgot the actual night because I borderline blacked out, but the narrative is quite infamous. Apparently, I hopped on my friend's tractor and started seductively grinding on it (why she had a tractor in our town, I have no idea), jumped in her pool and somehow forgot how to swim (while also thinking the green light she had in her pool was Medusa who was trying to drown me), and then ate double my body weight in half-microwaved Pizza Rolls in the name of munchies.

The more I partied, the more exposed I grew to the drunken charades of the hook-up culture. I'd watch my friends as they'd sneak off into empty bedrooms for a solid chunk of the night and prance back to the party gleefully exclaiming, *"So, who wants to take a shot?!"* And as each of my friends continued to harness their own powers of sexuality, I was watching like it was some kind of *National Geographic* documentary on human mating. I never got to experience it myself.

That was, until one drunken night I received that *"Hey new kid"* text.

Rachel took my phone and immediately started firing risqué messages back on my behalf. Within minutes he asked me to send a picture.

He asks for a naughty pictures before he even really knows you.

RATIONALIZING THE RED FLAG: *"He must really like me! Plus, he thinks I'm hot!"*

WHAT I SHOULD'VE DONE: Toyed with him and told him to use his imagination.

I FORGIVE MYSELF FOR: Losing my self-respect for a brief moment.

IF IT HAPPENS AGAIN: I will keep it classy and keep the guy dreaming about me.

SELF-LOVE LESSON: It's an earned privilege to have access to the most intimate parts of me, including a private look at me in a sexy ass bra.

Before I could even fathom what was happening, Rachel was instructing me in the bathroom on how to pose seductively in my fire engine red push-up bra and obtain the ultimate cleavage. Any self respect that I had for myself completely went out of the window at that very moment.

"*I can't believe I'm doing this!*" I nervously slurred to Rachel. "*I hope he likes them.*"

"*Bitch, you look HOT!*" she boasted as she added the perfect effects on the photo to enhance the contour of my collarbone.

After she pressed send, Seth instantly responded with exclamation points, hearts, and promiscuous pleas for more.

The following week my mom went on an out-of-state trip and I needed a ride home from my part-time job at the ice cream shop since all I had at the time was a driving permit. Seth graciously offered to pick me up after I posted a Facebook status asking for a ride. Man, the anxiety that I had that day at cheerleading practice before my shift… I knew *something* was going to go down. Would I… pop my cherry in a car? Or would we just kiss? Wait, how do I even kiss? (Do I make a zig-zag shape?) Am I overthinking this entirely? Some girls on the squad decided to give me a BJ crash course on a hairspray bottle that I carried around in my cheer bag as Lizzy watched and laughed. Can you imagine what our coach would've said if she saw us deep throating a bottle of Garnier and passing it around? I'm not sure if there's a specific policy anywhere in the high school handbook, but I'm sure that'd call for some kind of in-school suspension.

I made sure that I looked cute and wore a dress with some stockings for semi-easy access—at least that's what a *Cosmopolitan* article told me to do.

He picked me up at 8 p.m. in his Toyota Camry while wearing a plain black tee, basketball shorts, and a Yankees fitted baseball cap. The magazine did tip me off to the fact that if he was wearing basketball shorts, it was probably going to go down (though, in retrospect, I think a man would Harry Houdini his way out of any article of clothing if he knew he was about to get some). My palms immediately got sweaty (Eminem, I feel you) and my pits were heating up like a wood-fired oven. I awkwardly scuffled into his car as we simply started making small talk. Why is the weather always the go-to icebreaker? I will truly never understand that.

Although I didn't yet drive, I knew how to get home at this point. (Well, actually, let's pause there. I'm the most directionally-challenged person that you will ever meet—and I only know how to navigate by using food spots as landmarks. That being said, we were passing the McDonald's that was near the ice cream parlor across the street from that odd moss-colored building so I knew we were on track.) But then, he made a weird turn toward this park. That… was not the way. (And *The Mandalorian* would even agree.)

He doesn't go to the destination you agreed to.

RATIONALIZING THE RED FLAG: *"He must need to take a pit stop somewhere."*

WHAT I SHOULD'VE DONE: Asked if he was lost and redirected him towards my house.

I FORGIVE MYSELF FOR: Not verbalizing my concerns.

IF IT HAPPENS AGAIN: I will tell him I'd rather stick to the plan and go home.

SELF-LOVE LESSON: Listening to my gut instinct is an act of self-love. Using my voice is, too.

He then finagled his way down these creepily darkened streets that were sparsely decorated with flickering lights. He pulled over, put the car in park, and then turned off his headlights. He looked at me, blinked ever so gently, leaned in, and started making out with me. Honestly, I was so overwhelmed at the high-speed progression of it all that I just started writing the letters of the alphabet with my tongue (thanks, *Cosmo*). He moaned. I decided to start writing my name in script.

Then, I felt his hand wiggle his way down my shirt. He started tugging and squeezing and, for a brief second, I honestly wanted to pause and let out a, *"Holy shit this is happening!"* but I decided that would probably be weird. With his other hand, he took my hand and started gently grazing his groin. I could tell by the pulsations of the area that something was ready to come out and play—but this was all so foreign to me. I think he could tell that I was awkward or maybe not *that* experienced because I didn't make any other moves without his lead.

"Go on and kiss it," he seductively said as he pulled back from kissing me.

He then turned the volume up on his radio (which was a Yankees game), took his hat off, and placed it over the light shining from the dashboard as he reclined his chair back. I pulled his pants down as *it* just sprung out (almost like it was saying, *"SURPRISE!"*). I lowered my head, placed my mouth around the tip… and then I freaked out.

"I… I don't know what to do!" I frantically said.

"What do you mean? You've never done this before?!" he questioned.

"Well, I have! I've just… always been blackout drunk!" I lied.

"It's okay," he comforted. *"You just lick it like an ice cream cone… or a lollipop!"*

"I just lick it?"

"Yes, that's right. Like it's the yummiest thing you've ever tasted," he remarked.

"Sometimes, I chew my lollipops. Do… I bite it?"

He let out the heftiest cackle as if I had just recited a classic *Saturday Night Live* sketch.

"So, you're telling me you don't bite it like a Tootsie Pop?"

I guess to shut me up, he just took my head and shoved me over ***it.*** I kind of just moved my tongue around and based my skill level on the intensity of his moans. (Plus, every time the fans of the Yankees game clapped over a base hit, I felt as if they were cheering me on instead.) As I continued, the grunts got deeper and more frequent in nature. I felt ***it*** throbbing in my mouth.

I continued to lick his shaft as if it was a Fun Dip stick dunked in pounds of sugar. (To this day I'm not sure what turns me on more: the thought of sex or food.)

It feels like he's about to explode! I remember thinking to myself. *Oh yeah...*

He then confirmed my thoughts by struggling to say, *"I'm... about... to-oooo...!"* Before I knew it, the warmest, gooey-est, saltiest concoction of liquid vile projected itself into my mouth. I was, once again, overwhelmed. I always failed at beer chugging competitions. I took my mouth off of his nozzle and *it* profusely squirted all over my face and hair.

He smiled with relief.

His arm reached into his back seat as he grabbed me a sweat towel and said, *"Here."* (How romantic.) I proceeded to wipe his kids off of my face. I went to lean in to give him a kiss (look at me taking initiative!) and he said, *"Uhhh, that's gross."* It was at that moment I realized I still was flossing my teeth with his, uh, pubic hair. Probably not a good idea.

We drove home in silence. I got out of his car and said, *"Thanks for the ride!"* to which he replied, *"No, thank you!"* like a smart ass.

I got nothing out of this sexually myself—but what I did get was validation... and confirmation of my new equation: Men + me + going down on them = they want me! I'M WANTED!

The following day I felt unstoppable despite my face having been utterly violated and borderline graffitied like that of a Banksy wall.

"I'M THE BJ QUEEN!" I shared with all of my friends during the first block of classes. They all seemed to be so proud of me. That's one small step for my neighbor, but one giant leap for my womanhood.

For a moment, I traded my typical self-deprecating humor with my semi-scandalous storytelling. *"You know Seth? Yeah, that one hot outfielder who graduated? We hooked up last night!"* I told the girls at my lunch table.

I hopped and skipped up and down the hallways in celebration of my milestone. That was… until he texted me during my last class of the day. *"Why the hell are you going around telling everyone we hooked up?"*

He doesn't want anyone to know about your connection.

RATIONALIZING THE RED FLAG: *"He must be a private person."*

WHAT I SHOULD'VE DONE: Told him to keep his dick out of my mouth when he told me to keep his name out of my mouth— and then delete him from my phone and Facebook.

I FORGIVE MYSELF FOR: Incessantly texting him and offering him a BJ.

IF IT HAPPENS AGAIN: I will text a friend instead and move on from someone who treats me like a dirty little secret.

SELF-LOVE LESSON: I don't need to share my sex life with others to feel validated, but any man should be proud to have had an intimate connection with me (including a BJ).

"H-how did he find out?" I nervously murmured to myself.

I lied and said that I only told my one best friend. (Yeah, if the entire high school collectively counted as "one" friend, sure.) He rapid-fire texted me telling me that I was immature and to keep his name out of my mouth (which was somewhat insulting, considering where his dick had been the night before). He blocked me on Facebook moments later.

I crashed down from my high.

I texted! And texted him! And texted him! *"Please don't go! I'm so sorry! Please forgive me! I promise to go down on you any time if you just stop ignoring me! Please!"*

I got home—and the crazy set in.

I couldn't let my first high school crush slip away from me! My first kiss! My first BJ! What if this was your typical high school love story that just started off a bit, *errr*, messy (both figuratively and literally)? I couldn't let him go!

I volun*told* Lizzy to join me in my new private eye company which I founded to start heavily monitoring Seth's moves. He'd be outside playing basketball? Oh, how convenient, I needed to go on a walk and, uh, bird watch! He'd be working on his car? Nice, I just so happened to want to go for a little bike ride. (We genuinely thought we were skilled sneaks like Sherlock Holmes for no real apparent reason.)

Seriously, every single time Lizzy would come and pick me up in her beat-up sea foam green Kia whose passenger door was being hoisted up by some cheetah duct tape, we'd whip her car around the corner and blast this techno song that repeatedly stated, *"I can be a freak!"* just to make him feel like he was missing out on some action.

It failed—and made for some very awkward block parties where we had to pretend we were civil.

And to make matters worse, he started messaging some of my friends on Facebook and testing their boundaries.

Like I've said, I'm a Type A so I don't want to skip out of chronological order here—but I must admit, it was my mission, even years later, to complete the circle. Connect all of the sexual dots, if you follow. Similar to that Facebook message I received once I first moved in, once I finally moved back to the neighborhood post-college and post-break up from my one ex, I received a Snapchat notification that Seth has requested to befriend me. Moments later, it was followed by a shirtless picture with abs that looked like they were *trying* to peek out (but not really there) and text overlaying it that said, *"Hey new kid."*

I really had no shame after the adventures of college. Hell, I was practically known as the human vacuum my freshman year. (Okay, not really… at least I hope.)

More and more articles of clothing started to disappear. There was stroking. There was fondling. There were bodily fluids. Before I knew it we were sexting, but in fragmented nine-second video clips. It was wildly bizarre, but terribly hot.

The next day I messaged him to come over. Within seconds I heard footsteps running up my stairs—similar to that of a little kid's feet pattering toward the tree on Christmas morning to see the presents that Santa left. Except now I was the one to be unwrapped.

He spit his gum out across my floor (which, later on, I had to scrape off of my carpet… disgusting) and threw me on top of him. As I was straddling him and kissing his face, clothes were flying off. I rode him… except, I wasn't really feeling much of anything. I know I have incredibly thick thighs, so maybe that was just swallowing up the penetration? Or maybe it was the angle? Yes, that's it, the angle!

I then instructed him to switch positions and move behind me. This way, he could pretend I was a snare, and he could beat my back out like Nick Cannon in *Drumline*.

It was different than I remember. Usually, this position makes me *Scream!* like Drew Barrymore, but I wasn't really getting much of… anything. Maybe it's because he wasn't talking much (dirty talk really gets me going).

"*Talk dirty to me, Seth!*" I pretended to moan.

He shook his head no and proceeded to try and give me strokes. Okay, so I guess that's out. Maybe I just need him to ruffle me a bit.

"*Spank me, Seth!*"

I kid you not, I felt the tiniest, faintest little *tap* grace my cheeks. It was almost like Chubbs in Happy Gilmore: "*Just taaaap it in. Give it a little tap, tap, tappy.*" We weren't playing putt here, Seth. I wanted an actual bruise of an entire handprint to mark me for several days to come.

He tapped it again with the gentlest two fingers.

I mentally checked out.

"*Dear whatever higher power is out there, please let this end!*" I internally begged. He finished on my back about one minute later. He wiped it off with a sweat towel in the most nostalgic of ways and happily hopped down my stairs. Minutes later I received a text message with the thumbs-up emoji, the thumbs-down emoji, and a question mark.

I never responded.

I swore that was the last time I would ever reconnect with a past fling—or so I thought.

In full disclosure, after years of working on our maturity, both Seth and I have grown to establish a really dope friendship filled with mutual respect. He's a fantastic guy and I genuinely wish him nothing but love, happiness, and lots of roadside BJs.

Looking Within at Personal
RED FLAGS

- You don't set standards for behaviors that you tolerate from yourself—let alone from others.

- You jump into sex-related activities relatively fast... which includes sexting someone you barely know (nor can trust) rather risqué pictures.

- You allow your worth to be dictated by a popularity level.

- You openly (and even overly) disclose your sex life to others.

- You over-apologize.

- You correlate internal validation to obtaining external sexual activities (like I did with the BJ).

- You slightly stalk and/or become obsessive with a person that you're emotionally, mentally, physically and/or sexually attracted to.

- You don't take no for an answer.

- You lie about your sexual experience(s) to cater to the potential desires of someone else.

2

THE AWKWARD *AF* SLEEPOVER

Life can't be all play and no work—but it also can't be all work and no play. There needs to be a delicate balance, because otherwise, in my honest opinion, life is simply unsustainable. I never quite knew, though, that I could have play *at* work. This revelation (and HR-nightmare-in-the-making) just so happened to stumble my way when I started my first full-time job.

"Hey there, kitten tits!" greeted my training supervisor, Bradley, on my first day as he went in for a high-five after having just made our entire row of cubicles chuckle after telling a raunchy joke. *"I, uh, don't know what to train you on, so do you have any questions for me?"* He laughed as he sat down on the edge of my desk. *"By the way, is it alright if I call you kitten tits?"*

"That's a little late to be asking for consent, no?" I wittily snapped back. (This was the type of behavior that I used to encounter and expect from my old coworkers when I worked as a server, but I was definitely shocked to see this existing within a corporate environment. But, he seemed fun so I played along.)

"Ooooh, you're a quick one!" he said as he nodded his head up and down in approval of my banter.

"Kitten tits?" I laughed. *"That's aggressive."*

"There's worse… you got the Scissor Sisters over in that big office, Creepy Al to my right, my equally twisted spirit animal, Charlotte, sitting diagonally across from me, and Gay Bear Benji back there," he said as he introduced me to the workplace dynamics. *"He's not really gay, but he looks like something men would want to squish."*

Before formally accepting this role, my friend Melissa had warned me that her department was a little "crazy," but "like super fun and chill."

"And of course you know Melissa," he said as he pointed toward her desk to get her attention. I must've given her some kind of baffled *look* (I am the absolute worst at hiding my facial expressions) and she started cracking up.

"I'm entirely too hungover for this," I responded after having realized where the standards were set.

"You'll fit in perfectly," he joked. *"Welcome to the shit show. I'll show you everyone else as they trickle in."* (Duly noted, I could come late to work and no one would blink an eye.)

Now look, I shouldn't have given in to Bradley's sexual comments, but he was intoxicating in a *Wolf of Wall Street* way in terms of his confidence, sex appeal, charm, and business suave. He was 6 foot 4 with a sharply-trimmed auburn beard and he appeared to be in his early- to mid-thirties. He was responsible for his team of salesmen who essentially would sell print advertising and digital marketing opportunities, such as email blasts, pay-per-click (PPC) campaigns, and social ads to businesses in the area. Essentially, we worked at a mini marketing agency, and Bradley, of course, was in charge of some of the larger clients (and by larger I really just mean the more cash-invested ones). My role, therefore, was to monitor the campaigns and tweak them, as needed. For instance, if I noticed that certain keywords weren't performing as well in terms of clicks or leads, I would work with our data team to optimize the campaigns. I would also be tasked with compiling monthly reports and presenting these metrics to the clients in-person.

"I have no idea what I'm selling to these people so you need to make the dream come true," Bradley sarcastically stated.

I quickly learned that the dynamic of the operational structure was just as dysfunctional as the cesspool-like culture. For starters, two of our most prominent female leaders, Rayna and Toni, definitely seemed a bit too cozy with one another. There were rumors that repeatedly circulated my way that they were perhaps in some kind of secret lesbian lover relationship despite Toni being happily married for more than fifteen years with kids (at least that's the story that the pictures in her office portrayed). Then there was Creepy Al who most certainly lived up to his nickname after having tried to sleep with several interns and successfully swindling my other coworker, Aly, into somehow falling for him. Mind you, he was probably in his late forties, was in the middle of a separation from his significant other, and had a child at home while Aly was in her late twenties. This place was most certainly a movie—but the genre was still up for interpretation since it had characteristics of a comedy, porno, and something else in-between.

Bradley also shared scandalous stories of some team members who would allegedly do dirty deeds en route to client-facing meetings and somehow appear semi-put-together after getting tossed around in their cars like salads and reeking of foul play. In scouting through Bradley's team, there were two people I fantasized about getting tossed around with myself: Leo and Dane. As you'll come to learn, I have a weakness for Latin men—so that's how Leo immediately stole my attention. He was this dapper, physically fit papi with slicked back dark chocolate hair and a smile that would make even Dwayne "The Rock" Johnson do a double-take (and he has a stellar set of chompers). He came to work looking like he stepped straight out of a *GQ*

Magazine cover shoot and would always greet me in the sweetest, most sensual of tones.

"Hey there, Bri," he'd say as he complemented this statement with a soft wink.

My feline instincts wanted to pounce all over him. They grew even stronger once I learned that this thirty-year-old's entire body was covered in tattoos.

Then there was Dane who, like myself, was super nerdy. He had young features in terms of his chipmunk cheeks and soft, angelic skin. There was just something about him, though, that made me question if he was an undercover freak with his subtle, flirtatious smile. He had this teacher's pet type of mannerism to him—one in which I wouldn't be surprised if he somehow charmed the teacher into sleeping with him and then sneaked around and banged some classmates. All of these sex thoughts got me thinking that there must've been some kind of pheromones being pumped throughout the central air system of our office's floor. I was, and still am, genuinely concerned that if I ever took a blacklight to that office, I would've unveiled a sick amount of sexual secretions. Our master of chaos, Bradley—who was actually in a serious, loyal relationship—sat back and watched the sloppy reality TV show of our office film in real time.

It didn't help that our motivation seemed to be centered around the concept of partying, not purpose. I initially found it odd that quite a few coworkers seemed to get a little *too* happy during lunch hours and would basically spend the rest of their shifts once they returned to the office giggling at videos on their phones until the clock struck 5 p.m. (or sometimes even earlier just because they felt like it or wanted to keep the buzz going). Once I attended my first quarterly open bar outing to celebrate department-wide sales goals, though, I realized from where the proliferation of such behavior stemmed.

Dillon, our Director of Sales, rented out a local bar to thank our sixty-person team for not only meeting our sales goals, but surpassing them by more than $80,000 worth of contracts. Before we could indulge in the free food and booze, we had to sit through what appeared to be a presentation outlining our upcoming objectives. As his speech crept to the thirty-minute mark, I noticed how several of my colleagues appeared to get antsy. To me, the obvious shaking of their legs signaled that they were either starving and ready to ravenously tear up the pizza pies or they were desperately craving the sensation of booze as it trickled down the back of their throats. When the speech wrapped up and they all flooded to the bar, I srealized that I worked with several functioning alcoholics who could throw drinks down faster than I ever could—and I was practically fresh out of college. The shots started pouring, and, within two hours, I had to pause and ask myself if I was at a corporate work event or a frat party. I decided that I might as well re-enroll in college just for the night and pretend like I was back in one of those dingy rage basements while attempting to stomach the dollar store jungle juice. I got absolutely annihilated.

I recall wobbling over to my core group of work friends with some shots in hand but, in transit, I had to pass by a table that both Rayna and Toni were hunched over and leaning on. Rayna picked her head up, turned toward me, and said, *"Hey, Bri."*

"Oh, uh… hi Rayna!" I nervously replied after having never really interacted with her quite yet.

"You look like you're having fuuuuuun!" she slurred.

I blushed. I didn't know if I was too out-of-pocket for my first company event as I coddled several shots in my breasts to prevent them from spilling.

"You seem young and fun and…" she said as started breaking out in laughter, *"…question for you, has anyone ever licked whipped cream off of your chest?"*

All color completely drained from my face. *"Wait, what?"* I replied.

"Oh, I'm just teasing. It was a random thought," she said as she turned her head back to the table and laughed alongside Toni. Several nearby colleagues overheard Rayna's questioning and started cackling, too.

Bradley seemed to watch the interaction unfold. He walked over to me as I scurried over to my group of friends and said, *"See, there's something about those kittens,"* and laughed. *"I mean, damn, that was bold!"*

Your workplace is incredibly sexual in nature—and you contribute to the environment through your communication and actions.

RATIONALIZING THE RED FLAG: *"Ahhh, it's just lighthearted, playful banter... plus, we're all adults. I'd prefer this over one of those boring 9-to-5s any day!"*

WHAT I SHOULD'VE DONE: Recognized that entertaining and fostering these types of relationships—especially within the workplace—doesn't lead anywhere healthy.

I FORGIVE MYSELF FOR: Not only trying to fit into a situation, but fostering its growth as well.

IF IT HAPPENS AGAIN: I will set better, more professional boundaries.

SELF-LOVE LESSON: I can have fun in the workplace while also remaining professional and respectful.

"I need a shot," I said out of pure embarrassment, confusion, and terror.

"That's the spirit, bud!" Bradley laughed.

As I recounted the interaction with my coworkers later that night at the bar, Benji replied, *"Well, that's one way to quickly climb the corporate ladder!"*

We all started snorting from laughter as we normalized the chaos and molded to it as we pummeled back several more shots.

After a few weeks, I myself started to abuse the flaccid workplace structure knowing that there'd be no repercussions while HR personnel were sitting in their offices even more blind to the madness than Sandra Bullock in *Bird Box*. Even though the shift officially started at 9 a.m., I would wobble in no earlier than 9:40 every morning after getting plastered the night before with one of my best friends Scarlett. Knowing about the "shit storms" I would get into with Scarlett, Bradley would routinely approach my desk every morning to learn about what I had gotten into the night prior while I grunted in hungover pain from just looking at the brightness of the office.

"We love your spirit here," laughed Bradley.

"You know who I really want to love it?" I replied. *"Leo's fine ass self."*

"I'm on it, kitten tits!" he proudly stated. *"I would be honored if I knew that he painted a map of Hawaii on your chest."*

"Huh?" I questioned.

"Never mind, bud," he laughed. *"I'll wait until you're a bit more sober."* Bradley then walked away to finish making his rounds of R-rated morning laughter.

Once he escaped my peripheral, his statement smacked me harder than my need to vomit in the corporate bathroom: Bradley meant that he was going to encourage Leo to ejaculate on my chest. *He always has the oddest sexual colloquialisms,* I laughed to myself as I mentally acknowledged that he was wildly inappropriate but utterly hysterical. (I've never met someone else quite like Bradley.)

For weeks it was Bradley's mission to fulfill my fantasy. Leo would occasionally message me through our work chats and hit me with a few winky faces every now and then. Once he asked for my personal cell number, though, I knew that I was a few steps closer to some action. I was actually preparing for that moment for weeks as I accumulated a collection of semi-nude photos and stored them in my phone's photo library within a folder titled "Homework." (Honestly, who would want to peer into a document with that name? I thought it was genius.)

"Hey, new prospect ;)" he messaged me. (Why do guys seem to hit me me the oddest *"hey *insert nickname trying to be kinda-flirty-kinda-straightforward here*"* texts?)

Was he… trying to talk to me in Salesforce lingo? I let it slide until after a few exchanges he admitted that he wanted to *"closed won my pussy."* ("Closed won" is a sales phrase that roughly translates to a proposal having been accepted.) My lady parts dried up faster than the Sahara knowing that he was, indeed, flirting with me using sales jargon. At that point, I then pivoted my focus to Dane.

"I'm a little disappointed in my man Leo," Bradley stated. *"I was the Pippin to his MJ, and he let me down on the final dunk."*

We both laughed out loud as we exchanged equally as corny "closed won" statements. *"Truthfully, I was hoping that I'd get to see a picture of the kittens as a reward,"* he said as he shrugged his shoulders.

"There, there," I said as I comforted Bradley and patted his back. We had the oddest working relationship ever—yet I oddly loved every second of it. *"Maybe there will be better luck with Dane."*

It started with a quick follow on his Instagram. Dane posted relatively bland content in that it was mostly pictures of craft beer-filled pint glasses or nature shots. The feed started transitioning a bit, though, once he started taking up his new hobby: finger drumming. To this day, I'm still not exactly sure what the goal of this hobby was, but he appeared to have a mini drumming station and would beat his fingers to a rhythm of a song that he was attempting to produce. Dane must've had a proper station set up to film these interesting clips, too, because the camera lens focused ever so perfectly on just his hands—and never inched above the wrist bone—as they glazed over the padded buttons. It oddly turned me on.

"I wonder what those fingers do, thooooough," I joked to Bradley.

"I knew once you got comfortable we'd discover just how weirdly naughty you are," Bradley laughed back.

Dane and I didn't work together often, but Bradley did assign me to work on one of his client's reports out of fear of this business not re-signing. I put together a report that was beefier than a double-stuffed Chipotle burrito, and, boy, did that client bite in. By doing so, the client not only re-signed but added on several more marketing tactics—which propelled Dane and Bradley far past their quarterly sales goals.

A message popped up on my work computer later that day that read: *"Thank you so much!"* As I clicked to expand it, I realized that it was from Dane. Not even ten seconds later, he followed it up with: *"Drinks after work to celebrate?"*

And so, we met at a local Irish pub for what initially seemed to be just a happy hour. Our conversation started off rather awkwardly by discussing the weather while we both chugged our beers to feel a bit more relaxed. Naturally, our conversation then shifted gears as we discussed our mutually comforting grounds: the complexities and oddities of our department.

*"Wait, so she **really** asked about the whipped cream?"* he laughed as he gulped down more beer. *"I seriously thought that had to be a rumor."*

I got lost in the waves of our conversations as I surfed him all night long—metaphorically speaking, of course. Before I realized it, we had lined up the entire side of the bar with empty Guinness glasses. Dane snapped a picture and uploaded it to his Instagram stating that it was "rather impressive." We continued drinking until the pub closed. Having not left the seat for hours, I didn't realize just *how* intoxicated I had gotten—that is, until I stumbled off of the barstool as we were getting ready to leave and that wave of drunkenness completely tossed my head around like a tsunami.

"You definitely can't drive home," he said as he closed out the bar tab.

He drives while severely under the influence (which is also illegal).

RATIONALIZING THE RED FLAG: Honestly, I shouldn't have rationalized this. (And you should never, either.)

WHAT I SHOULD'VE DONE: Suggested that we call for a ride— whether that may have been either separately back to our respective homes or together back to his—and left both of our cars in the bar's parking lot overnight.

I FORGIVE MYSELF FOR: Making an incredibly risky decision that endangered my life and the lives of others on the road

IF IT HAPPENS AGAIN: I will call for an Uber or Lyft. There's literally no excuse for anyone to get behind the wheel of a car drunk—nonetheless for me to condone it and ride "shotty," either.

SELF-LOVE LESSON: Getting in a car with others who have been drinking has a far greater impact than one can probably imagine. I need to have a plan ahead of the night if alcohol is to be consumed.

"I can see if my friend Scarlett can get me!" I replied as I fiddled through my purse in the hopes of grabbing my phone. *"There it is!"* I confidently said aloud after I managed to hoist it out of my bag. I then squinted my eyes as I tried to de-blur the keypad—just before having it slip through my fingers and crash onto the sticky bar floor.

"Why don't you leave your car here, sleep over, and I'll drop you off here in the morning before work starts?" he suggested. (Mind you, he definitely shouldn't have driven, either.)

Once I walked up the stairs and entered into his apartment, my eyes were immediately fixed toward his computer setup in the far left corner of his living room, which hosted his finger drumming station. Methodically placed along his extended desk's surface were amplification systems, lighting fixtures, pads, and tripods.

What a nerd, I thought to myself. *Does he think he's going to be the Travis Barker… of finger drumming?*

My inner dialogue and light giggle came to a halt when Dane tossed a pair of basketball shorts my way and recommended that I change to "get a bit more comfortable." He then entered his bedroom, closed the door, and appeared to be changing, too, based on the sounds of drawers being ripped open and slammed shut. Once I finished switching my bottoms, I plopped onto his couch and wrapped myself up like a tortilla with his blanket. The weight of my eyelids dragged me into a quick, deep sleep.

I woke up to Dane's hot beer breath misting my face as he knelt in front of the couch only inches away. My eyes barely open, Dane fully went in for the kill and started attacking my face with the likes of his tongue. Practically unable to move from pure exhaustion and shock, I felt like a statue as Dane made out with me. Regardless, he moaned.

He started introducing words in between these sound bites as he muttered, *"Just touch it."* Simultaneously, he tried to take my hand out from under my body and place it toward his groin.

"What?!" I said as I tried to dispel the drunkenness from my body.
"Just touch it," he moaned again. *"Please, pleaaaase, just touch it."*

"Get away from me right now!" I yelled as I shot up from my horizontal position on his couch.

He tries to take advantage of you while you're under the influence (which is a crime).

RATIONALIZING THE RED FLAG: I'm proud to say that I didn't internally rationalize this one. Ladies, you shouldn't either.

WHAT I SHOULD'VE DONE: Did exactly what I did. Luckily this is not a red flag that I ignored, but I do know many ladies who have ignored it so I think it's important to point it out here.

I FORGIVE MYSELF FOR: Drinking so much. All the sexual stuff at work and the heavy drinking on a first date put me in a less-than-desirable situation.

IF IT HAPPENS AGAIN: I will be aware of how much alcohol I drink on a date. Also, I will no longer go to someone's home without being in full *sober* control of my own mental and emotional decisions.

SELF-LOVE LESSON: Drinking alcohol—when not abused—can be a fun and part of blowing off steam, but it should be done in a safe way with people I know and trust.

"This… this isn't what you wanted?" he questioned.

"I was just knocked out on your couch, Dane!" I barked back. *"Get the hell away from me!"*

I looked at the clock and it was nearly 2:30 a.m. With my phone dead and car still parked nearly half an hour away at the now-vacant bar, I ordered him to go into his room before I shouted so loud that his neighbors heard and called the police.

"I figured you wanted to touch it!" he said. *"I misread the signs... I'm sorry."*

I scurried through his musical play area for a charger as he pitifully putzed to his bedroom door. Once my phone was juiced up enough to power on, I ordered an Uber home. I had only a few hours left to catch some z's before I had to Uber myself back to the office and figure out a way to get to my car.

"You look terrible, kitten," Bradley commented as I slugged my way over to my cubicle and crashed into my chair the following morning. *"Long night?"*

"Yeah, I went out for one too many drinks last night," I shared.

"Where'd you go?" he questioned.

"Oh, just this local Irish pub," I vaguely responded.

"Which one?" he pressed.

"It's too early for this interrogation, man!" I huffed back. *"But if you must know, I went to Mac's Pub."*

"Waaaait a second, wasn't Dane there, too?" he said. *"I saw him post a picture of quite a few beers and tag that he was there."*

"SHHHHH! Not too loud!" I shared.

As I clung to my chair, he rapidly rolled me into one of the smaller conference rooms and asked about the finer details of the night. Once story time came to a close, he burst out laughing and said, *"My new nickname for you is M.C. Hammer."*

"Wait, why?" I said.

"Because he can't touch this!" he sang as he did his best attempt at the Hammer dance. *"Listen, you gotta tell the crew this one!"*

Like Bradley boasted, I shared this semi-laughable horror story with my immediate work friends later that day. Immediately, they all started referring to him as Pepé Le *Pervy* Pew.

"Between this and the whipped cream, you're a living legend here!" Benji laughed.

Then it hit me: I didn't want this to be my legacy. Being violated in and out of the office and adding to the #MeToo statistics was not what I ever envisioned nor dreamed of when I formally accepted my bachelor's degree and pledged to take on the workforce. This department most certainly had its moments of crooked laughter, and I did form some of my greatest friendships to date (Bradley, I'm talking to your wild self), but I knew deep down that personal and professional growth was not possible in this type of environment.

Determined to better myself, I eased back on the weeknight party lifestyle and started brushing up my résumé. I ramped it up in my graduate classes and started partnering with the University's Career Services Department in search of my next opportunity. When I finally landed another full-time job after the laboriously tedious interview process, I felt like a snake who had just shed her skin. I could be a new woman.

Up until my very last day, my coworkers would continually spam my text messages and emails with gifs of M.C. Hammer dancing.

"You know, we were going to send you off with a pair of parachute pants as a farewell," Benji said. *"But, we figured you'd rather have one last wild lunch-time happy hour, on us."*

"I thought full-time jobs would be a bit more, well, put-together," I said to Benji as I chewed on my half-priced buffalo wings.

"HA!" he said. *"Man, adults can be worse than kids."*

And, boy, was he right.

Looking Within at Personal
RED FLAGS

- You don't shut down any hypersexual talk in the workplace and/or your own actions have contributed to an oversexualized atmosphere. (Sure, it may seem fun in the beginning, but those environments often devolve into a mess.)

- You don't respect yourself enough to know when to walk away from a person or situation.

- You drink entirely too much when out on a first date (or even during a work function).

- You rely on liquor to dilute feelings of stress, anxiety, fear, or even discomfort.

- You allow your late-night behaviors (i.e. drinking or partying) to affect your punctuality, professionalism, and promptness.

3

Rap-PED UP

I guess we're comfortable enough with one another for me to just come right out with it: I have a sexual kink for Michael Myers. No, not the guy who plays Austin Powers. (I'm sorry, but I don't want to shag you.) I mean the sociopathic serial killer who emerges on Halloween to demonize the residents of Haddonfield. (You on the other hand, yes.) There's just something about the way that he aggressively chokes people that gets me all riled up. Clearly, I thrive every October 31st. Naturally, when I saw a Latin man out one night at a club with a tattoo of Michael Myers on the top of his hand, along with an entire gore-themed sleeve, I basically died… and then was resuscitated… and then died again.

It was my friend Emma's birthday weekend and she coerced us all into clubbing for the weekend in Atlantic City. (For clarification, by coerce I mean that she simply asked us if we'd like to join her and we all immediately responded with, *"HELL YEAH!"*) We packed our most provocative outfits and headed down the parkway for our getaway in the hopes of grinding on men all night long as they bought us drinks. I made Scarlett tag along with me to ensure that the maximum potential of excitement was achieved.

Scarlett has been one of my best friends since my early twenties. Imagine if Rihanna and Uma Thurman's Poison Ivy character had a baby—yeah, that's how utterly beautiful she is. She has these big, juicy, succulent lips that make any man swoon, these devilishly enticing green eyes, deep cherry chocolate hair, and a perfect hourglass body. There's also this spontaneous, fiery side to her that dominates any room that she is in and complements her physical looks so effortlessly. At the club (or any nightlife scene for that matter), she is the life of the party because she's always dancing and encouraging others to get rowdy. After one too many drinks, though, she tends to fall into one of the following buckets: overly flirty or overly aggressive. Her overly aggressive side tends to come out when she's in a mode of protection. If someone makes a slick or mean comment about one of her girls, it's game on.

I actually got into my first and only bar fight with Scarlett. It was while I was working at that toxic corporate job. We went out for beat-the-clock Tuesday at this lively bar that everyone flocked to on this particular night because at 8 p.m. the beers cost only $0.25. Every hour after that, the price would increase by another quarter. After having thrown back nearly one dozen beers at this point for under $5, Scarlett needed to go wait in line to use the restroom, which wrapped around the entire perimeter of the bar. As she waited in line, I would yo-yo back-and-forth to the bar to properly supply us with drinks. Once we approached the front of the line and were moments away from entering the physical bathroom, two sloppy females pretended that their friend was in the bathroom and that they "needed to help her" (classic line) as they giggled amongst themselves.

Scarlett asserted her dominance and said, *"Hey, we've been waiting in line for like thirty-five minutes."*

"Yeah, fuck off," the drunk girl slurred back.

"What did you say to me?" Scarlett snapped back.

"You heard me, bitch!" she said. *"Fuck off, we're next."*

Other females waiting in line immediately started provoking the altercation by chanting, *"WORLDSTAR! WORLDSTAR!"* (For those of you who don't know, WorldStar is a content-aggregating video blog site that mostly shows videos of people fighting, dancing, or doing something to elicit a reaction.)

The one drunk friend slammed my friend against the wall. Her comrade then secured her fingers around Scarlett's neck and hoisted her off the floor as her feet dangled in the air. I saw people start to whip out their phones and press record as they aimed their cameras toward Scarlett practically levitating off of the ground. Something within me just *snapped* and I rushed over. I threw the one girl who had Scarlett by the neck into the bathroom and knocked her into a garbage can that rested right beneath the sink. I then pushed the other girl out of the way into the crowd. With the main perpetrator now lying on the ground, I began vigorously kicking her with the precision and power of an MMA fighter. I blacked out from anger— and it actually terrified me knowing that I had that within me. I just kept kicking and kicking and kicking until I finally felt a hand on my shoulder pull me back.

"Bri, I really need to use the restroom now," Scarlett giggled as I looked and saw that I was the only one fighting.

"How long… have I been doing this?" I questioned, a bit frightened.

"Long enough," Scarlett laughed. *"Now let's go!"*

She then waltzed over to the stall as if nothing had just happened, and I followed behind her. As she was taking her turn, we heard knocks on the bathroom door: *"SECURITY! YOU NEED TO GET OUT!"*

"What?!" Scarlett responded. *"We were attacked! We need to leave?"*

"Ma'am, we can't have people doing that here, self-defense or not," he asserted. *"You need to leave the bathroom now before I come in and take you out."*

This angered Scarlett. *"Well, I'm peeing, so you're gonna have to wait!"* she responded.

As we flushed and exited the stall, the security guards told us that we needed to "stop playing around" and leave immediately. This riled Scarlett up, who then walked toward the sink to wash her hands.

"I told you I wasn't playing around, ma'am!" the security guard said as he approached her, flipped her over his shoulder, and fireman-carried her out of the restroom. Another security guard then escorted me out of the bathroom. We were banned from coming back to that bar for the remainder of that year (despite the fact that there were no serious injuries and no charges were pressed by either party).

As you can imagine, it's always a whirlwind of a night with Scarlett—and I love the adrenaline. Outside of that environment, though, she is one of the most responsible, nurturing, and loyal individuals that I have ever been blessed enough to know or to call a friend. For this upcoming club-filled weekend in Atlantic City, though, I fully anticipated (and encouraged) wild Scarlett to let loose.

When the group of us arrived at our hotel, we did the ol' pregame-while-you-get-ready strategy, meaning that, by the time we finished doing our hair, makeup, and changing, we were already quite buzzed. I put on this long-sleeved, deep v, cut-out fire red dress that strapped around my body in such a way to hide my lower belly pooch and accentuate my legs. I complemented this with a smokey eye and a bold red lip to match the color of the outfit. Of course, I popped on the 6-inch nude heels with the gold chain that wrapped around the ankle for the finishing touch.

When I looked in the full body-length mirror, I honestly was turned on by myself.

"Damn, I genuinely feel like I look hot tonight!" I confidently said as I slugged back a shot.

"Girl, you always do!" Scarlett laughed. *"Stop talking about yourself like that!"*

"Scar, I'm channeling the confidence and sex appeal of Kim Kardashian tonight," I said as I smiled back at my reflection.

"Take that energy to the club and let's land you a hottie," Scarlett said.

We headed over to the venue and started doing what we do best: drinking and dancing as if it were our jobs. We weren't even there for thirty minutes when Scarlett provoked the attention of one "flashy" guy who appeared to be in his late twenties or early thirties. He suavely approached her with his Gucci shirt, belt buckle, and shoes and, of course, a gold Rolex that sparkled every time a laser beam pointed in his direction. She disappeared over to the bar and then brought me back a drink.

"Yes girl, keep doin' your thing!" I whispered in her ear so as to not let the man know our playbook.

As she was dancing a few sections over from me (but within my line of vision), I proceeded to throw my dump truck of an ass back and show off my dress with our other friends. For the first time in a while, I felt like one of the hottest women in that club. About a half hour later, Scarlett's man approached me.

"Hey, my friend wants to come over and talk to you," he shouted above the music, *"but he doesn't know if he's your type."*

"Oh yeah?" I smirked. *"Which one?"*

"That one over there in the glasses," he said as he pointed over to his group of friends and identified the hot Latin man.

"Tell him to come over," I said.

He went over and encouraged his friend to talk to me—and brought back Scarlett and the rest of his friends in the process. Scarlett quickly approached me before the rest of the herd appeared.

"Bri, he looks like your papi lumberjack!" she snickered.

Papi lumberjack (*noun*): My ultimate fantasy of a Spanish-ish man who I can envision rocking Timberland boots with plaid shirts while adorning a big, burly (but beautifully manscaped) beard across the purest and softest of smiles; looks like he could chop some wood and then tear my kitty up while rolling his r's ever so softly in my ear. (Woof, I'm getting riled up.)

"I mean, he's dressed up right now, but giiiirl, I can definitely see it, too," I smirked back.

As he stepped closer, my attraction grew. He, too, was displaying the Gucci logo on his eyeglass frames and black shirt, and he paired that with black jeans that ripped at the knees and some sleek dress shoes. His ripped arms were covered in tattoos, which immediately weakened the strength of my lower body. Then there was his sharply trimmed beard that I just wanted to sexually yank.

"Lady in red," he said as he smiled. *"You caught my attention the second I walked in here. My name is Berto."* Even in my six-inch heels, he was taller than me. Check mark.

"I'm Bri," I responded. *"I love your tattoos... especially this one,"* I said as I pointed to the Michael Myers mask on his hand.

"I'm a Halloween freak," he laughed.

As people were twerking and grinding around us in the middle of the dance floor, we had our own little bubble of a conversation. I learned that he lived only about forty minutes away from me in an apartment by himself, had a full-time job as a manager of a tattoo shop, was into music, lost a significant amount of weight by going to the gym, and doesn't go out much but because of his boy's birthday he made the exception. As he spoke and his mustache hairs danced around his mouth, I noticed that he had a bit of a scar on his lower lip that almost looked like a battle scar from a fight.

Oooh, a bad boy, I thought to myself.

After a while, he'd caress my hand and whisper spicy statements into my ear: *"You look so fucking good, mama."*

I'd thank him for these compliments by slowly grinding on him. Every now and then, he would try to turn me by the waist so that our faces would align and lean in for a kiss—but I would tease him by pulling back, rubbing my hands up and down his biceps, and encouraging him to work a bit harder.

Without even realizing it, the night approached 3 a.m. and the DJ made a few announcements that we only had a few songs left. Berto whipped out his phone and then asked me to give him my number. When his phone lit up, it unveiled his lock screen: a picture of a newborn.

"Aw! Is the baby yours?" I questioned.

"Yes, I was going to eventually tell you," he said. *"I'm a father."*

"Oh, wow!" I remarked. *"This must be an old picture because the baby looks so young here! How old?"*

"He's about three months old now," he said.

"Oh!" I said.

"He is my whole world, and I was going to tell you… I was scared it might've shoved you away, love," he said.

"What about the mom?" I questioned.

"It was a really bad relationship, and she tried trapping me," he assured me. *"We're not together… she's crazy."*

"Oh," I once again said.

"Let me take you on a dinner date next weekend when I don't have the baby and let me explain," he suggested.

I quickly chugged the remainder of my drink just before the club's lights turned on. I looked over at Scarlett who was sucking her man's face—and she gave me this *look* that she wasn't ready to call the night quits just yet.

"Do you girls want to come back to our room for a bit to drink?" Scarlett's man asked once he walked over and talked to me. *"It'll be me, Berto, and my boy Drew, and we can just drink and maybe even head to the casino downstairs after."*

I looked over at Scarlett with questioning eyes. My inner sex-deprived kitten wanted to go for some potential foreplay action, but my logical self knew that we should stay with our original group.

He calls his ex "crazy" without elaboration, clarification, or a deeper discussion.

RATIONALIZING THE RED FLAG: *"Everyone has a crazy ex, no? He just so happens to verbalize it."*

WHAT I SHOULD'VE DONE: Known that he was probably the crazy one.

I FORGIVE MYSELF FOR: Getting caught up in the moment and being hypnotized by my Michael Myers fantasy.

IF IT HAPPENS AGAIN: I will call him out and walk away.

SELF-LOVE LESSON: I must remember, whatever he does or says about an ex he will likely one day be doing to or saying about me.

"Come on, Bri, let's just go for a few," she urged. *"We don't have to stay long."*

That was all it took to officially convince me. Berto held my hand as we walked with them to their room as he continued to whisper steamy statements into my ear and rub his tattooed hand up and down my back.

As they opened the door, we entered into a suite with two king-size beds, a balcony view of the city, and a massive bathroom that had a whirlpool bathtub. I sat down on the bed closest to the balcony and immediately ripped my heels off to alleviate the throbbing pain after having danced all night.

Berto was just finishing putting on some background music when he questioned, *"Oh, do your feet hurt mama?"*

I nodded my head.

"Let me help with that," he added as he walked over with a red Solo

as they asked for more details. They were particularly fascinated and confused by Drew's role in the night. (I still am to this day.) Later that afternoon as we made our way back home I received a text from Berto saying, *"Hey gorgeous… I'm just waking up now ;)"*

For the next week, Berto and I talked daily—even at work. My one coworker, Natty, actually saw me smiling as I feverishly typed away on my phone, so she questioned who the lucky guy was on the receiving end. When I told her that I was talking to a literal daddy, she paused and questioned what I was doing.

"Girl, I don't know… but he's so damn fine," I laughed.

"You wonder why you've yet to find your person," Natty said, *"but you devote your time to these dead-end roads. But girl, let me tell you, they do make for some funny friggin' stories."*

"See, I'm just trying to have fun!" I dishonestly said as I had a pile of pictures of ten possible men, including Berto, stuffed into a folder on my desk ready to bring to this love psychic later that evening in order to tell me, based on the "feelings" that the photos were emitting, if I've yet to find my soulmate. (Thankfully the corporate printer didn't jam up and print at a later time because that would've made for an awkward explanation as to why half-naked men were left in the print tray. Oh, and in case you were wondering, none of the photos "spoke" to her, and I've yet to find "the one." Yeah, so, anyway, my psychic probably questioned my own energy after that session, to be completely honest.)

I jokingly told myself that maybe the steak that I was promised to indulge in that Friday with Berto would be my twin flame and, after all, who would I be to mess with the universe's calling? So, I drove to his apartment to meet him prior to then traveling together nearly half an hour to this highly acclaimed restaurant in the city. Prior to my departure, Scarlett asked that I share my location with her so that she could track my exact whereabouts just in case something went wrong.

"You sure you want to do this?" she texted me.

"It's too late now!" I voice-to-texted her back as I made my way there.

"Yeah, I see that," she said.

When I arrived at his apartment, he told me that he'd walk to my car and escort me to his apartment "just to be safe." He approached the driver's side, whipped open my door, voluptuously kissed my lips, and masculinely gripped my hand as he guided me toward his place.

"Glad you got here safe, beautiful," he smirked. Damn, he smelled even better than he looked, too.

Once we approached his front door, he commented, *"Welcome, my lady in red."* As he swung his door open, I immediately noticed that baby toys were scattered all across the hardwood floor.

"I'm sorry about that," he laughed as he loosely kicked a light-up sensory toy out of the way. *"It's been a crazy week."* He then proceeded to scurry across the floor and pick up rattles, squeaky toys, and binkies and place them into a bin near the far left corner of his living room.

"It's okay," I awkwardly laughed. *"I mean, it's not like we'll be staying long anyway!"*

"Actually, I was thinking maybe we could get to know each other a bit more and order in instead," he stated.

"I mean... I was really looking forward to steak," I responded.

"But think about it, we can watch a horror movie, relax on the couch, and chill," he convincingly stated as he then walked over to his refrigerator, pulled out a bottle of Grey Goose, and then mixed us two vodka and club sodas with lime. To quickly alleviate the awkwardness, we both immediately chugged the first drink. Without hesitation, he proceeded to pour us seconds. Then thirds. Within twenty minutes of entering his apartment, I was now three triple-shot drinks deep.

He walked over to his television and appeared to be searching for a flick, which I assumed was the reasoning for the "you can get comfy on the couch" statement. Instead, he let out his next big secret.

He nonconsensually manipulates the situation to his benefit.

RATIONALIZING THE RED FLAG: *"He just wants to get to know me better without the distraction of dinner."*

WHAT I SHOULD'VE DONE: Insisted we stick to the plan. I mean, damn, didn't I learn this already? Plans changing are a massive red flag.

I FORGIVE MYSELF FOR: Trying to be easy-going instead of demanding what I want and know is a healthier way to build a real relationship.

IF IT HAPPENS AGAIN: I will say no to anything less than the plan I was expecting.

SELF-LOVE LESSON: Dating is essential to get to know someone before jumping to the bedroom. Sex can be wonderfully intimate—and intimacy should then happen in the mind first.

"So, when I told you I was into music back at the club," he said, *"I really meant that I was a rapper with over ten thousand followers on Twitter."*

"Oh," I said. *"That's, uh, cool!"*

"I wanted to give you a little peek into my art," he said as he pressed play to his first show—and rapped along. Every few seconds, though, he would pause the video and break down the meaning of each bar because he wanted to ensure that I understood what he was saying line-by-line. This continued as he explained three different songs.

"Them lines go hard, don't they?" he said as he then looked in the mirror and gave himself a little wink.

"Yeah, I can definitely appreciate it," I said. *"Hey, do you think maybe we could order something now?"*

"Those drunk munchies hitting, love?" he laughed as he then pulled

out a late-night fast food menu from his junk drawer. *"How about some cheese fries, mozzarella sticks, and chicken fingers on me?"*

I should've listened to that love psychic. As he picked up the phone to dial-in the food, I excused myself to the bathroom so that I could vigorously text Scarlett and explain my predicament of the uncomfortable ego-boost of a rap performance that I just had VIP front row tickets to. She told me that I should stop drinking so that I could sober up enough and drive home, but I knew I would be unable to drive until the morning. I self-admittedly confined myself to the decision of having to choose between either getting an Uber home (which would have been well over $200) or spending the night.

Once I exited the bathroom and replanted myself on his couch, he then asked questions about my work, passions, family, and friends. Though the topic of family was mentioned, he never seemed to address the situation regarding the mother of his children—even when he promised to have that conversation. (Quite frankly I knew that our "relationship" was not going to escalate past this night so I didn't care to keep pressuring him to disclose such information.)

"Tell me a funny story about you," he commented as he took another gulp of his drink.

I told him about the time that I hitchhiked back to my dorm room in college after a house party was broken up by the cops after someone pulled out a machete (no, I'm not kidding) and threatened to slice her boyfriend for dancing with some other girl. I ran out of the house along with Kayleigh, my roommate, and Ryen, our mutual friend, to avoid any legal complications for underage drinking. We attempted walking the three miles back to the halls in the middle of a snowstorm. (Mind you, Kayleigh and I were wearing mini skirts, crop tops, and six-inch heels and were not properly equipped to truck through this tundra.) The three of us discussed ordering a taxi, except none of us had any cash on-hand. We genuinely thought that we were going to freeze to death until we saw headlights pop-up in the middle of the road. As the car slowly approached, we saw an illuminated Domino's sign on top of the car appear within the whipping winds carrying the heavy snowfall. Ryen flagged the car down and encouraged the driver to roll down the window as he pleaded to get a ride home. Initially, the driver declined the proposal. However, once Ryen started rapping along to the Wu-Tang Clan song playing over the driver's radio, the driver had a shift in mindset and agreed. Though getting saved from potentially ending up like Jack Nicholson at the end of *The Shining* could be argued as being the highlight of that encounter, mine happened to be that I was able to accompany the driver on a delivery and personally hand a customer his pizza pies.

"*Godddddamn!*" Berto laughed out loud. "*Mama, I think you have mine beat!*"

"*Oh yeah?*" I remarked. "*Let me hear yours.*"

Berto then reapproached his TV, opened the YouTube app, and typed in "WorldStar" in his browser. He scrolled through the sea of videos until he clicked on one titled "*Rapper Gets Skull Cracked After Show!!!!*"

"*Yeah, so I've been jumped three times because some people can't handle the fire that I spit,*" he laughed as he glanced over at the television. "*Two of the videos are actually online, and they give me a good laugh.*"

My eyes were glued to the screen as I watched this thirty-second clip feature someone sneak up on Berto from behind after a show in Detroit, clock him on the head with his fists, and pummel him into the concrete as a member of his crew filmed it, and shouted, "*HARDER! HIT HIM HARDER!*" Berto laid on the ground in a puddle of blood unable to move.

"*That's how I got this scar right here,*" he said as he pointed to his lip. I knew it was a battle scar, but he redefined that term rather literally in this case.

He sadistically boasts about violence.

RATIONALIZING THE RED FLAG: Yeah, there's no rationalizing this shit.

WHAT I SHOULD'VE DONE: Told him that I'm not in any way, shape, or form turned on by violence (except, of course, for Michael Myers) and insisted on leaving the situation.

I FORGIVE MYSELF FOR: Even being at his place in the first place.

IF IT HAPPENS AGAIN: I will not listen if someone jokes about violence. Period.

SELF-LOVE LESSON: The things people are proud of give insight into what they value. Am I aware of what I'm proud of?

I continued to drink in fuller force knowing the mess that I was neck-deep in. For the remainder of the night, he continued to hold the conversation hostage as he discussed topics that I genuinely held no interest in. After a certain point, I just wanted to shove my foot in his mouth to quiet him up. I settled for him leaning in to kiss me so that I could at least hold his tongue hostage now. Though I held no attraction to his personality, lifestyle, or behaviors, I had the drunk munchies and I wanted to eat his body. (Clearly the cheese fries did not hold me over.) He grabbed my hand once more and took me to his bedroom.

I wanted to stop right before we had sex and selfishly relive the foreplay action from the club the weekend prior. Instead, when he whipped my pants off and made my legs rampantly shake with his tongue again and—in the moment—asked if he could feel inside of me, I obliged. It wasn't anything that spectacular for me to go into detail about, especially being that I was more fixated on getting it on with my circadian rhythm than with him. We ended up falling asleep next to one another once he finished.

When I woke up the next morning to leave, he appeared to still be in a deep slumber while he snoozed on his side facing the wall directly opposite of his bedroom door. I softly tapped him a few times to try to wake him up and say goodbye, but when he didn't answer I decided that I would lean in and whisper that I was leaving so as to not be rude.

"What the FUCK ARE YOU DOING?" he yelled, startled, as he woke up and tried to backhand slap me away from his body. Thankfully, I reacted in such a time that I ducked out of the way and pulled myself back.

"I was just saying goodbye... what the fuck?!" I responded.

"Who the FUCK does THAT?" he yelled. He then rolled over and went back to sleep.

I stormed out of his apartment and called Scarlett in a state of confusion. I told her about the night, and she inquired, *"Girl, why did you even stay?"*

"Scar, I... I really don't know!" I said while angrily holding back tears. *"I should've left once I got there and the plans switched up, but I dunno..."*

"Uh, Bri..." she sighed.

"I can't believe he did that to me..." I said back to Scarlett as I sat down in my car and then paused to collect my thoughts. *"I'm going to text him and go off!"*

"Wait, why?" she questioned. *"He's not even worth it."*

"I don't know, but that was fucked up," I said.

"Don't do it," Scarlett said.

"Too late," I said after having already typed half of a paragraph.

Scarlett continually tried to enforce the principle in my mind that it'd be a waste of time. I disagreed, though, knowing that I, too, could use my "art" of writing to battle his God-like complex. One text wasn't enough, though. I sent him another. Then another. Then another. I wanted him to reflect on each line like he made me do in watching his videos.

"You know he doesn't care, right?" Scarlett said.

"But I do!" I said. *"You know what? Fuck this! I'm going to call him and tell him off!"*

Abruptly, I hung up the phone with Scarlett and immediately started dialing Berto. He declined my first call, which fueled me with more hatred. I called him again. That, too, was declined. I called back Scarlett in a frenzy.

"What did you honestly expect from him?" Scarlett asked.

"I literally… I… I don't know," I sighed.

"You need to respect yourself more to not have put yourself in this situation," Scarlett responded.

"Girl, you do the same shit, too," I said as we both laughed.

On that drive back home, I repeatedly told myself that I needed to do better. Well, at least now I can almost cross off my bucket list the fantasy of getting sexually strangled by Michael Myers—that is, if by a hand with his face tattooed on it counts.

Looking Within at Personal
RED FLAGS

- You view yourself solely as a sexual object.

- You don't listen to your gut.

- You easily grow an attachment to anyone and everyone in your life.

- You need validation from a man in the form of physical touch.

- You hook-up with someone that you hold absolutely no attraction to... just because you feel like you're "stuck" in a situation you can't get out of.

- You continue to drink (and rather heavily) to blur your decision-making and make you feel not-so-guilty about being in a particular situation or environment.

- You expect respect from people who have shown nothing of the sort.

and these big, brown eyes that would uncontrollably and visibly shift from side to side (she had a vision disorder that eventually self-healed over time). Nonetheless, I admired her beauty. We bonded like the molecular structures we learned about in class—and became inseparable.

We'd call each other every night after 9 p.m. as that's when the minutes were free (the early 2000s were truly something else). We'd hog up the phone lines for as long as we could. That is, until her grandma would eventually kick us off and tell us rascals to *go on and get to bed!*" Every single weekend we were together as Lizzy would introduce me to the likes of Johnny Depp films, pop-punk music, and cheerleading routines. She typically wore all black and the only pop of color in her attire was this huge, sparkly cheerleading bow that she'd wrap around her ponytail. She also introduced me to makeup after having learned to apply layers of thick, black eyeliner just below her lower lash line. Over time, we discovered that we grew up with very similar family dynamics—and so our connection grew stronger. Her sisters became my sisters, and we basically gifted the other with second mothers.

As middle school progressed and technology advanced, she became my number one friend on Myspace and my T-Mobile Fave 5. It was literally me and her against the world of our hometown, spending nights together at the movie theater, mall, and skating rink. No one could infiltrate our bubble—not even the pubescent boys who started to grow an affinity toward Lizzy. You see, Lizzy grew more beautiful with age—and I just, well, grew in size. I was terrified that once we entered high school, we would drift.

Our freshman year Lizzy started to venture out and befriend some of the skaters who were known for being "wild" and partying in the local park once the sun shied away. Our daily hangouts started to grow sparse as Lizzy started exploring attention from some of the cuter, badass boys. She eventually started to date this one emo kid with side swept dark hair named Blake and even started drinking and smoking—which shocked my core because I viewed her so purely and innocently. I was so heartbroken by her transition, jealous of her admired identity, and upset by this abandonment that I basically ignored her for the next year. I, once again, found solace in my schoolwork and ended up fostering friendships with fellow nerds.

Practically best friend-less and thinking that I'd be vulnerable to more cruel comments in the new environment, I decided that if I started to make fun of myself before anyone else could, I could get the people laughing *with* me and not at me, right? (Alright, I'll admit, it wasn't a healthy mechanism, but it temporarily worked.) People started to fall in love with my self-deprecating jokes and klutzy mannerisms. So, I took my hilarity and lack of athleticism to the freshman softball team. I was decent. Let's face it, I couldn't really slide into a base (instead I sort of just *plopped)*. I did have one mean arm to throw, though, and when I did make contact with the ball up at bat, I'd send that bad boy soaring. Really, though, I just pepped up my teammates, hooked everyone up for the games with sunflower seeds for the next few years, and made them laugh as I took balls to the face during practice. (I guess you can say my first teabagging was in the ninth grade.)

The beauty of playing softball was that during the official season I would shed weight. Though I was still bigger than most of my team-mates, I was a bit more solid (and not as floppy) during those springtime months. After all, I had to run one mile in under eight minutes to officially join the team. When I would start to feel a bit healthier as a result of my activity levels, I would go into this anti-gluttonous extremist behavior in which I would only eat the smallest portions of the cleanest and leanest of foods to keep the momentum moving. It was during this stage of my life that I realized I would either undereat *or* overeat—and there was absolutely no in-between or sense of moderation. Like I said, I've always had an unhealthy relationship with food that I still battle to this day, but it was during this period that I realized I could swing into either direction like that of a pendulum. Once the season would come to an end, I would return to what I like to refer to as hi*BRI*nation mode and eat like I was prepping for that of a cold, long winter (even though it was the start of summer).

Some of my superficial family members grew concerned that I could start to get bullied again for being a butchy, bigger softball player—so they heavily encouraged me to try out for the cheerleading squad for that feminine balance. Let it be known, though, that I can't even cartwheel (but I do have one majestic forward somersault, if I do say so myself). Out of fear of being ridiculed, I dragged my uncoordinated self to the tryouts and somehow made it to the team for the rest of my high school career. I hated cheerleading with a passion—especially how the flyers would spring off of my base-like body and constantly leave my arms scattered with bruises. That, and how our uniforms looked like they were straight out of a 1970s catalog. (Coach C, you had a terrible eye for fashion—but somehow you always had an eye out for my long acrylic nails that you yelled at me to cut down for four years.) Whatever, at least I loved being reconnected with Lizzy. Balance, am I right?

So, like I was saying, I masked my insecurities with extracurricular activities and humor—and that's how I exponentially grew my circle of friends. Eventually everyone knew me: the typical jocks, studious nerds, popular preps, over-the-top theater kids, edgy punks, chill stoners, class clowns, abstract artists, aspiring rappers, mean girls, and even the sex fiends. I connected with every one of them on different levels as we basked in my peculiar comments and witty jokes. My strategy seemed to pay off when I was voted the Funniest Woman by popular vote in the yearbook. (I almost won Homecoming Queen, but someone printed out one of my Facebook statuses poking fun at my chemistry teacher's clown-like makeup, and I was told that I could no longer be crowned the title because it wasn't very role model-ish. A few of my friends wore shirts with my name on them during the ceremony to make me smile and metaphorically give the finger to our principal.)

My "popularity" particularly springboarded after junior year when I befriended Rachel, who was one of the most well-known and liked girls in my graduating class. She was, and still is, one of the most beautiful, intellectual, caring, and loving of individuals whose heartwarming smile always complimented her chocolate eyes and golden silk-like skin. We bonded over our "interesting" humor, love of handwritten notes, and philosophical conversations. Though she was most certainly blessed with a body that I think even the likes of Jennifer Lopez would be a bit envious of, she somehow always managed to make me feel beautiful and loved in my own skin whenever I was in her presence. Her friendship opened my eyes to this feeling of equality, self-acceptance, and happiness. Balanced in nature, Rachel introduced me to this concept of work-life harmonization. For juniors in high school, this simply meant both excelling in school during the week and chugging warm Natty Ices out of a beer funnel on the weekends. She also woke up this dormant sexual dragon within me comparable to the one from *The Hobbit* (except instead of craving gold, I craved all the boys).

I yearned for external validation to nourish my soul—except after a while, I started to realize that I was never actually full. Sex, parties, and other temporary "fixes" will never satisfy the insatiable appetite that exists when you don't truly love yourself at your core.

THE RED *Room*

- What key lessons did you take away from Part I?

- Did you ever fall for any of the red flags that I fell for in Part I? If so, which ones?

- Did you notice any red flags that I didn't point out in Part I? If so, what were they? What might you have done in that situation?

- Have you ever pursued someone that your friends told you not to go after? If so, why did you still do it?

- Have you ever "blown up" a person's phone begging for attention and answers? If so, what did you hope to achieve?

- Have you ever relied on liquor to help you hook-up with someone? If so, why?

- Have you ever correlated a sexual touch (or even just attention) to your own personal worth? If so, why? Where does your worth come from for you?

- Has a sexual encounter ever given you a false sense of validation? If so, what do you believe are the root causes of that for you?

- Were you ever bullied? Do you think that has impacted the way that you view yourself… even years later? Reflect on the experience.

- Do you or have you ever suffered with body dysmorphia? If so, how has this affected your romantic (or even raunchy) relationships?

- Have you ever made fun of yourself to avoid people making fun of you first? How did that make you feel?

- What's your relationship with your diet and nutrition like?

- Are you a person that tends to become easily "attached" to someone that you hook-up with? If so, why do you think that this may be?

- How can you create and maintain healthy boundaries with sexual and romantic partners moving forward?

Part Two

ROLLER COASTER

[rōlər ˈkōstər]

NOUN

a thing that contains or goes through wild and unpredictable changes

RELATIONSHIPS

[rəˈlāSH(ə)n͵SHips]

PLURAL NOUN

the way in which two or more concepts, objects, or people are connected, or the state of being connected

5

THE CHERRY ON TOP

I know it seems like several years of my life were this messy blur of booze-induced bizarreness. I'll be honest, the weekends for a while most certainly were—but it was almost as if I lived this double life. This behavior started in my later high school years and really ramped up from there. You see, my teachers all knew me as the hardworking intellect who was crushing concepts of imaginary numbers in college-level calculus and interpreting the rhetoric used in classics like *Gatsby* in advanced literature and language arts. My Sunday-through-Thursday diet was textbooks, but then my second identity would sneak through on the weekends and required nothing but pre-portioned liquid meals of fermented wheat (aka beer). It was in this period of my life that I learned the artful skill of balance. (I said artful, not healthful.)

Despite my party antics, I still managed to graduate within the top 10 of my high school class of nearly four hundred students. I almost earned a near-perfect 4.0 GPA, but that one B+ in world history left its dent. (Mr. Williams, I still don't forgive you for that.) My mom had aspirations of me going to an Ivy League school (and I was even accepted into the one that I applied to), but I barked back, *"I don't care about college!"* Weird for a bookworm, right?

The application process was grueling in and of itself. Mentally, I was checked out after having to write my first essay over a topic that, quite frankly, I didn't care about. (I sound like such a bratty teenager.) But that's not the *real* reason. I'll be honest: I was happy. Utterly, undeniably happy. I didn't want to face the reality that my high school days were soon inching toward an end—and I didn't want my bubble of happiness to burst. It took me nearly two years to finally feel accepted and "in"—and I feared starting over at a completely new campus with a community of people who might very well judge me. I could only imagine the remarks I'd get with my curly bob haircut, questionable fashion sense, laughable smokey eye makeup, kangaroo pouch of a beer belly, and cackling hyena laugh.

But, of course, I had to finally accept that we'd go our separate ways come the late summer and that we all had to, well, grow up.

To quiet my mom, I formally accepted my offer to attend an in-state private university. It was near a beach, close enough to come home on the weekends, if needed, and had its own radio and TV stations. I thought, *Hey, maybe I'll be the next Jon Stewart whenever he leaves The Daily Show!* (Curse you, Trevor Noah.) The biggest deciding factor, though, was that the university was throwing scholarships my way like confetti given my academic standing. Basically, the first two years of my undergraduate career would be completely covered. The remaining two? Eh, I figured I'd think about it when I got to that point.

So cool, I had a plan… that entailed me moving off and being separated from Lizzy, Rachel, and my other friends. Lovely.

Let's party and delay these thoughts, I'd think to comfort myself.

So that's exactly what I did. I partied. Even harder than before.

One notable night was coordinated by my friend Perry. He lived in this beautiful house on the mansion-esque side of town. His pool was shaped like an actual dolphin. (I thought only celebrities had the means to do something as exquisite as that.) After about eight beers to the face each, me and the girls belligerently jumped into the body of *Flipper*, grabbed a floaty, and chilled. That was, until we heard what sounded like the largest mosquito of all time getting zapped to smithereens. While practically snapping our necks to look toward the sound, we noticed a group of guys circling one individual who was being crowned by a blue iridescent light. The zapping started again followed by shrieks of, *"Dude, is he really doing it?"*

"No waaaaaaaaaaaay!" another shouted.

The crowd slowly peeled back, unveiling this guy from my high school class with his swim trunks below his knees, left testicle in his left hand, and taser in the other. Yes, he was electroshocking his own ball. It was like a car accident—you didn't want to look, but you genuinely couldn't break your eye contact. The craziest thing was, this guy didn't budge. He took it to the sac like a true sociopathic champ.

This was the first impression of my now-best friend, Charlie, who I'm pretty sure that night performed his own vasectomy. The next party I saw him at, the dude came dressed up like a full-on pirate and kept calling everyone "matey." For those of you wondering, no, this wasn't a costume party. He was outlandish—yet I knew I needed that energy in my life. (Welcome to the thought process of Brianna in her late-teen years.) I couldn't wait to bring him around to college parties and piss off—or totally impress, depending on the night, I guess—some of the fraternity bros.

Knowing that I had to now branch out of my comfort of my eclectic hometown friendships, I joined my college's Incoming Freshman Facebook group in order to acclimate myself to others. I quickly learned who the "hot" girls were (and who would probably pledge themselves to a sorority), the beloved athletes, the popular party boys, and all of the other social circles. Amidst the flurrying fleet of social posts and pictures, I felt lost. I knew that I would need to somehow find my circle again—and I was terrified.

As the weeks crept by and the buzzing of Facebook notifications from this group continued to intensify, I did end up connecting with this one girl named Anne. She was this grounded, well-structured, intelligent, and curvaceous dirty blonde who was excited to party but not get "too overly crazy." I needed someone like her to reel me back into focusing on my academics if I started to inch a bit too far over the rowdiness line. Although she wasn't going to dorm in the same building as I was, our campus was relatively small, so we decided that once we moved in, we would familiarize ourselves with the culture together.

That first night post-move-in, Anne and I heard whispers of a party at one of the boy's soccer houses off-campus. The words "boys" and "free liquor" within the same sentence was enough to convince us to pop our "college party initiation" cherries. I put on my shortest mini skirt, black stripper-esque eight-inch Jessica Simpson zipper stiletto heels, crop top, and smokiest of black eyes and headed to Anne's dorm to pregame just a bit before we called for a taxi to the party. I invited my roommate to join me, too, but she wasn't quite into the partying scene (so, as you can imagine, we drifted slowly apart as the semester rolled on). I formally met and hugged Anne once I walked into her dorm where she greeted me with a shot glass full of cheap liquor. Together, the two of us slugged back a few quick shots—null of any chaser for half an hour—and then decided to call a taxi to head out for the *real* party.

As any college student would do, we poured the remainder of the vodka into an empty water bottle so we could continue drinking en route to the party, headed down to the parking lot, and hopped in our ride with our driver who we came to know as "Teeny Todd." Teeny Todd apparently was a living legend around these parts. He was this big, fluffy, older guy with a burly white beard who resembled Santa—and being that it was only September, I was sold on him being "the man." Although he made quite a few inappropriate sexual jokes, he allowed us underage college students to openly drink liquor in his car, so we let it slide.

As we turned onto the street of the party, we joined the conga line of dozens of other taxis that were stopped in the middle of the street unloading hordes of drunken college students. There was even a queue to get into the party that snaked around the outskirts of the house—and every time the appointed "doorman" would let people into the house, the music would escape from their sound-proofed walls and permeate through the air.

"Am I drunk or are our seats vibrating from that bass?" I laughed to both Anne and Teeny Todd as another group walked through the house's side door and I simultaneously slammed the final vodka shot back.

"You're definitely drunk, but even my seats are vibrating… and I'm a big boy!" Teeny Todd said as he laughed even harder.

As Anne and I exited the car and inserted ourselves as pawns in the waiting game ahead, anxious thoughts started to infiltrate my mind: *What if I wasn't hot enough and I couldn't get in? What if the doorman thought I was too overweight to enter? What if I embarrass myself by being the worst dressed in the party?*

"Bri, are you okay?" Anne said as she nudged me and woke me out of my trance.

"Oh, yeah, sorry about that… I just zoned out," I lied. *"Girl, let's rage!"*

The line moved relatively quickly. The doorman appeared to be keeping a tally on the occupancy and guests' levels of intoxication prior to entering—and he also handed us our personal red Solo cups to drink out of for the remainder of the night. Once we finally made our way into the house, the two of us followed the sound of the bass as if it were our travel guide into the basement. As we descended down the creaky stairs into the darkness, we were guided by neon signs and lights that eventually led to the party's dance floor rimmed by kegs.

"Girl, we made it!" I said as I danced to techno music blasting over the DJ's speakers in the far left corner.

"HELL YEAH!" she shouted above the music. *"Let's drink!"*

We approached the one soccer boy who was manning the keg and maniacally pumping it as if it needed CPR. We shoved our cups under his nozzle as he filled us up to the brim. Anne and I clanked our cups together and chugged to the sound of Steve Aoki's "Turbulence." As the beat dropped, the team would start jumping up and down and smacking the beams that spanned across their basement's ceilings along to the rhythm. I feared that the floor above us would cave in as more and more debris seemed to fall with each bass drop, but then I stopped overthinking and joined in on the riot.

The more that we jumped, the more beer that spilled. Within minutes of us being at the party, Anne and I noticed that our shoes were starting to not only stick but sink into their sludge-filled floor like quicksand. I guess you could say that we quickly learned that we were to never wear shoes that we adored at college parties as they would get destroyed in the same capacity as our livers.

We also noticed how the upperclassmen (and I mostly mean the guys) would appear to be scoping out the freshman class as they waited to pounce and make their kill for the night. After all, our college was relatively small in terms of population. (I myself even grew to know practically everyone on campus within the first few months of party-ing.) I assumed that the upperclassmen wanted a different "taste" of the semi-innocent and curious freshmen to break away from the cesspool of hook-ups from the previous year. We were new blood, and these vampires were thirsty.

And so, to make us freshmen girls feel "loose," the older boys encouraged us to do keg stands (especially the more attractive ones who wore mini dresses).

He's not only encouraging excessive alcohol consumption, but he's filtering who he encourages said alcohol consumption to based on looks alone. (In other words, he's treating certain females differently based on their perceived levels of provocativity, "sluttiness," and overall sensuality.)

RATIONALIZING THE RED FLAG: *"He thinks we're hot! Whatever, drink up!"*

WHAT I SHOULD'VE DONE: Probably not have flashed my hoo-hah to the party while doing a keg stand for the sake of wanting to impress upperclassmen strangers and to feel accepted.

I FORGIVE MYSELF FOR: Indulging a little (...too much, actually).

IF IT HAPPENS AGAIN: I should be aware of what I'm wearing and how I look while also determining whether or not a guy is making advances towards me based on my appearance alone.

SELF-LOVE LESSON: I can wear whatever I want, but I should be conscious of someone's motives for getting me to drink.

They quickly intoxicated all of us with the constant pouring of cheap beer. In fact, one of the freshman girls got so drunk that she went to take a swig out of the decorative Bacardi bottle that was filled with water and highlighter fluid thinking that it was some kind of unique, glow-in-the-dark flavor. She quickly had to be escorted out of the basement after dry-heaving and, to my later understanding, was left outside in the backyard covered in her own vomit without her friends since they were too preoccupied by the attention of men at the party.

Anne and I, too, were distracted as we danced all night and eyed out the men on our "wish lists."

"Look at him over there with the Steelers hat!" I shouted. *"He's fiiiiiiiiiiiiiiiiine!"*

"He's all yours!" she said. *"I want that guy over there with his biceps all out and looking like a snack."*

Our fantasizing came to a halt once we heard the rampant running down the stairs by one of the soccer boys as he shouted, *"THE COPS ARE HERE! CUT THE MUSIC!"*

"EVERYBODY RUN!" the DJ shouted over his mic as the lights turned on and the soccer boys attempted to move the kegs into a hidden closet.

I looked over at Anne in a state of utter panic and confusion. There were dozens of people trying to hide under the DJ booth, behind locked doors, and even in hidden closets within the basement. My fight-or-flight instinct kicked in, though, and I knew that we had to leave. This fear was amplified once I heard the police upstairs barge through the front door and assertively yell at people attempting to leave to *"STOP RUNNING AND GIVE US YOUR IDS!"*

I noticed a few of the younger athletes shimmying out of a window in the bathroom basement and sprinting out of the backyard before the police swarmed that route. I looked over at Anne, and we instinctively agreed to exit in the same fashion. We stepped on the grungy toilet and hoisted ourselves up while practically scaling the wall to fit through this half window. Once we both somehow managed to escape, we noticed flashlights bouncing up and down around the corner of the house as the police tried to catch the rest of us from escaping. The only way to free ourselves was to hop the ten-foot fence toward the end of the backyard and run.

"BRI, LET'S GO!" Anne shouted at me as I froze in fear at the thought of potentially getting ticketed for underage drinking on my

first night of college.

"BUT I'VE NEVER HOPPED A FENCE!" I shouted back as I drunkenly made my way toward the fence. *"I DON'T KNOW IF I'LL MAKE IT!"*

"Just throw your whole body over it!" she shouted back as she straddled the top of the fence and tried to lend me a hand.

My first two attempts were failures. I actually ended up falling, scraping my knee, and busting the heel off from my left shoe. The cops started to close-in as they yelled, *"YOU! BACK THERE! DON'T MOVE!"*

"Come on, Bri!" Anne urged.

I took one more look at her, took a few steps back, and then accelerated in full-speed toward that fence. I managed to somehow find just the perfect foot placements in my half-functioning heels and crawl up that fence like a gecko. I reached the top, exhaled in relief, and then looked down as I noticed the drop I now had to make.

"GET DOWN FROM THERE!" the one cop shouted as he and his partner approached the fence and threw his hands up to try and reach for my foot.

With no time to further think, I jumped. Except, I didn't realize that my left hand was caught on the spiked post cap, causing the inside of my palm to completely rip open. I was now gushing with blood.

"Bri!" Anne said. *"Oh my god, are you okay?"*

"GIRL, I JUST HOPPED MY FIRST FENCE!" I replied as I went to high-five her with my oozing hand.

"Let's not use that hand for now!" Anne joked.

The two of us whipped our heels off and wobbled the two miles back to our dorm room as I tried to apply pressure to the wound in my hand. We laughed as we exchanged stories of drunken nights back in high school and then disclosed personal information to solidify our newfound friendship.

"*I wonder when we'll start hooking up with men,*" Anne said.

That's when I embarrassingly told her that I was still a virgin.

"*That's not anything to be ashamed of!*" Anne said. "*I actually just lost it my senior year of high school with my boyfriend at the time.*"

"*I always thought I was this crazy late bloomer,*" I said.

"*It's on your time,*" she said as I smiled back at her with relief, "*and no one else's.*"

We continued to maneuver through the darkness of our college town with no GPS available. Once we saw our school's neon mascot light illuminate through the night like an oasis in a desert, Anne and I excitedly picked up the pace knowing that all we craved were our beds—and some Tylenol to hopefully curb the impending hangover. We approached our buildings, which were separated only by a walkway, said our goodbyes, and then walked into our respective dorms. I was so happy to be back that I didn't even realize that I was literally leaving a trail of blood behind me. (I would've definitely lost a game of hide-and-seek at this very moment.)

"*My girl, are you okay?*" a man sincerely questioned as he puffed out his cigarette while leaning against the side of our building's entrance alongside my two other future best friends, Luella and her cousin-roommate, Belle. "*You're looking a bit rough.*"

"Yeah I, uh, I need sleep," I responded to the then-stranger.

"*Where's your room?*" he questioned. "*Let me walk you up,*" he said as he threw the cigarette butt to the ground and crushed it with the tip of his shoe.

"I… I don't even know," I drunkenly responded.

"*Let me help you,*" he said as his face then welcomed the most comforting and wholesome of smiles. "*My name is AJ, by the way, and I'm one of the girls here,*" he added while he took his left shoe off, removed his sock, and wrapped it around the palm of my hand almost like a bow.

"Ow!" I responded to the added pressure. *"I'm Bri and… I'm a hot mess,"* I laughed.

"Let me walk you to your room," he said as he did a little twirl to commemorate our new friendship.

Together, we meandered through the hallways as we attempted to locate my room. In conversation, we discovered that we both shared an 8:30 a.m. philosophy course with our first class being the following morning. He joyously promised that he would come to my room within the next few hours, wake me up, and walk with me to class.

"Girl, no more hopping fences if you ain't that agile!" he laughed as we approached my room on the third floor with my nametag on the door. He gave me a hug, kissed me on both cheeks, and wished me the sweetest of dreams.

Though I initially felt hesitation in joining this college's community in fear of being an outcast, I felt peace knowing that I quickly was forming relationships. (Although Belle later revealed that I looked like an absolute "animal" that night, which was clearly a great first impression.)

AJ, Belle, and Luella started to join Anne and me in our late-night adventures. Partying was an easy way for me to meet friends. Naturally, I'd say that I can woo anyone with my ability to converse, but in a party setting when I'm drunk, my "walls" fall as I find comfort in being my authentic self, who, for instance, can't really dance but doesn't care because I'm having a grand time. I definitely took it to the extreme, though, when I started to go out every single night and oversleep for a majority of my morning classes. It didn't matter what day of the week it was: we always found a frat house, sports house, or general upperclassmen house to satiate our thirst for more beer. It also didn't phase my professors when I spewed out laughable excuses to try and explain my absences and tardiness… which resulted in point deductions. These grade penalties eventually reflected in my midterms and finals. For the first time in my life, I saw nothing but B's and B+s, which was completely out of my bookworm-like character. (At the time, it felt like the sacrifice that I needed to make in order to make friends.)

All of the binging gave me a hearty reality check not even one month into the semester when the freshman fifteen [pounds] quickly attached to my body. Cue the body dysmorphia bells for this next phase of my life, too… *ding ding!* While Belle, Luella, Anne, and others would wear the skimpiest of dresses and cut-out clothes and look damn good while doing it, I tried to stay on par with my miniskirts and belly shirts—except I didn't feel confident, skinny, or sexy enough. I masked my insecurities by submerging my digestive system into a pool of beer and, once again, playing the character of "the funny girl who everyone should love only platonically because she'll make you laugh."

After only a few weeks, it started to feel reminiscent of my high school self as my friends created sexual connections while I sat back and observed from a distance. I longed to be touched, wanted, pursued, and craved. This sensation began to overtake my body like a viral infection—and the only cure seemed to be sex.

Eventually I embraced my liquid courage and would begin making out with guys almost weekly whose basic criterion was to give me attention. Clearly, I didn't set the benchmark very high. It got old quickly, though, once I realized that after the sloppy exchange of saliva, there'd be very little communication post-hookup unless, of course, we unexpectedly ran into each other at another party and gravitated toward each other like inebriated magnets.

"I want to be desired!" I exclaimed to Anne as we talked in my room and nursed our queasy stomachs. *"It seems so easy for everyone else… I feel like a loser."*

"You just need to believe that you're sexy, which you are, and then show it!" she said. *"You know, and then feel confident flirting!"*

"I don't want there to be a sequel to The 40-Year-Old Virgin and they cast me as the lead," I said as I masked my sadness with humor.

"Oh my god, Brianna, shut up!" she laughed as she lightly smacked my arm. *"Alright, I can see this reaaaaally is starting to bother you, and I get it. But stop beating yourself up!"*

"I want someone by like Halloween," I desperately demanded. *"You know, to pop my cherry in a sexy costume!"*

"Okay, that's an oddly specific request in a rather aggressive timeline!" Anne laughed as she realized that was merely three weeks away. *"You're determined as hell!"*

Every night thereafter was a mission like that of *The Witcher* video game. I would chug my liquor, enter a grimy party, and peruse the area for my attempted longer-term hook-up. Although it's sad to admit, anyone with a penis, nice smile, and decent sense of style was fair game at this point—though I, of course, had my sights set out for one of the hotter and more popular guys. So, as you can imagine, when one of the star football guys gave me the *look* at a party only a few days later, I basically felt like I popped my own cherry from squeezing my legs so hard in an attempt to prevent my Hoover Dam from breaking. With only his eyes, I was turned on... and pretty much soaking.

I couldn't *not* know him as his name was constantly projected by the announcer's voice multiple times throughout a home game for completing some kind of miraculous play—and we'd hear the crowd chant, *"LET'S GO MARK!"* even from our dorm rooms on the opposite side of campus. Out of curiosity during one of the quarters, I scrolled through the University's website to locate the roster. There he was: this incredibly tall, handsome upperclassman with a sharply kept crew cut and taper fade. His arm was adorned with black and white traditional tattoos. My ovaries were screaming his name louder than the sports commentators.

He was so fine—which made me question, *"Why is he looking like that at me?"*

I tried to give him that *look* back, but my lack of confidence broke the direct contact as I quickly shuffled my eyes in another direction. But, just to be sure, I then quickly looked back and, to my amazement, there he was in all of his glory staring directly into my soul and biting his lip. I softly took a sip of my beer, gave him a smile, and then turned toward my group of friends.

"*Guys, I think that hot football guy is eyeing me,*" I blushed.

"*I think he's actually making his way over here,*" Belle excitedly said.

"*Wait, wha—...*" I attempted to speak for clarification until I felt a hand tap my shoulder.

"*Hey, I couldn't help but notice you,*" he said. "*You have such a beautiful smile,*" he added as he, too, smiled.

I blushed, and my chest broke out in nervous hives. "*Oh, uh, thank you,*" I bashfully said. "*You do, too.*"

"*I've been seeing you around at a few of these things,*" he said. "*You should hit me up some time on Facebook.*" He then took his phone out, opened his Facebook app, tapped on the search bar, and instructed me to type in my name.

"*Brianna,*" he said as he followed the flow of my fingers, "*I hope to see you soon,*" he added right before he walked back toward his group of friends.

I turned around to face my girls who were trying to refrain from jumping up and down. I was surrounded by *OMG*-s and *GIRL NO WAY!*-s for several minutes. I, myself, couldn't believe that I just exchanged information with one of the hottest upperclassmen I have ever laid my eyes on.

"*You need to wait until tomorrow to accept his request,*" Luella suggested. "*Don't look too thirsty!*"

"*Oh, I know something that she wants to suck on to quench her thirst,*" Belle wittily added.

"*Goodbyeeeeee,*" I jokingly said as I chugged the remainder of my cup. The rest of the night, I was drunk off of endorphins.

That next morning I ventured over into my Friend Request inbox and immediately accepted his invitation. As most women do (or at least the ones that I surround myself with), I stalked his profile. He mostly posted football stats and highlight clips from the games with the occasional sprinkling in of "boys night out" pictures. I did notice that his comment section was filled with heart emojis from dozens of other women. There was one female in particular who would always comment *"That's my baby<3"* with other decorative smileys on every single post. Did he… have a girlfriend?

I ran over to Belle's room to showcase his profile and analyze in unison.

He's flooded by comments from females on social media as they try to claim him while he, himself, appears single.

RATIONALIZING THE RED FLAG: *"It's not his fault that he's so damn hot and everyone wants to claim him as theirs."*

WHAT I SHOULD'VE DONE: Realized that they were claiming him because he was making them feel like they were his.

I FORGIVE MYSELF FOR: Being charmed by the attention.

IF IT HAPPENS AGAIN: I will take it super slow and ask him about it.

SELF-LOVE LESSON: I have to know my worth and radiate confidence and positivity, not mask it with alcohol and men. Self-love is a state of appreciation that grows from actions that support our physical, psychological, and spiritual growth.

"Do you know how many fangirls he probably has?" Belle rhetorically asked. *"He's never posted about her and has never responded to her comments as far as we can see,"* she added as she scrolled through his feed and viewed content from months prior.

"Oh, yeah, good point!" I said in relief.

"Get out of your head!" she said. *"Now, wait a bit to see if he'll message you."*

Not even five seconds after Belle made that comment, I received a notification that Mark had messaged me a smiley emoji. Both of our mouths dropped and then, at the same exact moment, screamed as we then grabbed each other's hands and jumped up and down and spun around in a circle on her tile floor. (I now half-sincerely apologize to her downstairs neighbors.)

Belle took my phone and let her charm do the talking on my behalf. It was small talk, yet packed with a flirty punch, for several exchanges—which prompted Belle to then take a more aggressive approach once he wasn't providing a concrete action plan:

"So, are you going out this weekend? I'd love to run into you ;)" Belle said, disguised as me.

"I won't be going out for about two weeks hun. I have a big conference game coming up," he said.

"Bummer," I said aloud to Belle, but then paused as I saw that he was still typing.

"I'll be going out Halloween weekend tho so let's link up then," he replied.

My next mission commenced: find the sexiest, sluttiest, and most alluring costume that Party City could sell within the budget of my measly on-campus job, which paid $6.15 an hour with a maximum workload of nine hours per week. Knowing that I needed to be a bit more creative, I settled rather last-minute on a cliché provocative cop mini dress with fishnet stockings and fake leather fingerless gloves. I then paired this with dollar store handcuffs that I'd cusp around one of my belt loops and my infamous stripper heels that I wore out nearly every night. (I'd even swing the handcuffs around my finger and practice my strip tease as Belle laughed and called me an idiot.)

"I just want to handcuffed and fucked real good," I said as I anticipated the night to come.

"That's like, a level three request, and you're not even past the first level, girl… pump your brakes," she said as we both laughed out loud.

"So like, how drunk do I want to get for the occasion?" I asked Belle.

"Enough to feel loose, but enough to remember your experience," she responded.

The two of us somehow scrounged up enough money to split a bottle of Everclear (which, for those of you who have never drunk this, do yourself a favor and keep that streak going). Though utterly disgusting in flavor, this alcohol most certainly allowed us to teeter on that line of blacking out, but not *quite* tipping that point, within just a few shots if we calculated our tolerances accordingly. Belle used her sexual desirability to convince one of the upperclassmen track boys, Niko, to do a liquor store run for us and, with this bottle as a token, grant us our self-coined admission into our Drunken Hoe-lloween Freakend.

While Niko grabbed our bottle, Belle and I headed to the dining hall and filled up some empty water bottles with chasers from the beverage dispensers. I chose a pulpy orange juice while Belle pursued the carbonated route. Regardless, we knew that these liquids would barely mask the pungent taste of our 151 proof grain alcohol. We timed it so that we'd arrive back at our dorms just as Niko would be dropping off our bottle.

After we obtained the 750 ml bottle, we started getting ready: Belle dressed and sang like Britney Spears in "Baby One More Time" as I, well, pretended to be a sexy cop issuing a warrant for Mark's arrest. In the middle of our back-and-forth banter, my phone buzzed as I received a text message from my roommate saying that she was heading home for the weekend to hang out with her high school crew for their annual party.

"Uhmmmmm, this couldn't have aligned more perfectly!" I said aloud.

"This is your moment," Belle slyly said, *"so seize it!"*

I took a shot out of excitement—and a few more while we continued to get ourselves together. Then, of course, we had to take one for the road as we hopped in Teeny Todd's taxi and headed to the track boy's house for their banger. As we left our dorm's parking lot, several other taxis picked up packs of students, too.

The taxi drivers shouted out of their windows, *"Hey! Where ya headin'?"*

"Green street!" Teeny Todd shouted back. *"You too? Must be a wild one tonight!"*

Our college neighborhood was amazing in that, even if you didn't know the actual address to a house party, as long as you followed the flood of other taxis you'd find the coveted location. As we approached the drop-off point, I somehow spotted out in the distance Mark making his way through the house's entrance.

"OH MY GOD HE'S HERE!" I exclaimed.

"Wait, did you see?!" Belle questioned. *"He's dressed like a cop, too!"*

"There's about to be some kinky things going on tonight, ladies!" Teeny Todd inserted. Though creepy and unsolicited, he was right in that the roleplay fantasy was heightened.

And so, we said our goodbyes to Teeny Todd and made our way into the heavily crowded front lawn and maneuvered toward the doorman for our ritualistic red cup. The music was booming so much that I felt as if I had front row tickets to a rave. It was madness—and I couldn't wait for it to infiltrate my being. Literally.

It was difficult to move once we found a spot in the basement given the load of people in the room. To shuffle our way over to the keg and squeeze in through the little nooks between sweaty partygoers while getting smacked by awkward dance moves took an astounding thirty minutes and then, to hopefully find and reunite with our group of friends after, took even longer. Though it was packed and the music was jumping, after about two hours Belle and I gave each other that *look* and knew that it was too crazy to move, nonetheless mingle. We agreed that we'd rather go back and party in the dorm with whoever stayed back.

As we snaked our way through the crowd, I felt a hand grab me and pull me back.

"Misses Officer, nice to see you," Mark said as he winked.

"You have good taste," I replied as I eyed his costume up and down.

He leaned over and nuzzled his head against my neck as he whispered, *"That's why I want to taste you later."*

He goes right to sex within minutes.

RATIONALIZING THE RED FLAG: *"He was just giving me what I wanted... why else would I have dressed up like the sexy cop?"*

WHAT I SHOULD'VE DONE: Not texted back.

I FORGIVE MYSELF FOR: Turning right to sex to feel better about myself.

IF IT HAPPENS AGAIN: I will do things that truly nourish my mind, body, and spirit so I feel good from within myself first.

SELF-LOVE LESSON: My body is a temple. Period.

"Ohhhhh my GODDDDD, you are so sexy!" I wanted to scream. Instead, I felt Belle yank my arm and hoist through the crowd toward the exit. *"TEXT ME!"* I yelled over the bobbing heads.

"BIIIIIIIIITCH!" I said to Belle as we finally could speak within a normal decibel level. *"Mark wants to TASTE ME!"*

"Girl, LET HIM!" she said as she embodied the ultimate hype woman. *"GET! THAT! SHIT!"*

"Oh my god, oh my god, how do I make this happen?" I panicked.

"Text him your room address with a winky face," she replied. *"Be assertive and go after it!"*

I listened to her plan. As we made our way back to our dorm through another taxi ride, my phone buzzed with a new text message notification.

"It's Mark!" I shouted.

"Open it, open it!" Belle said back. *"I'm excited and I'm not even the one getting the pipe!"*

"He said that he'll be there in twenty!" I shouted back to Belle.

"Okay, okay! Calm down!" Belle said as we scuffled out of the car and into our parking lot. *"You have the perfect amount of time to freshen up and take a few shots! This is perfect!"*

We ran up to my room and performed a pre-cunnilingus cere-mony: we fluffed my pillows, sprayed my ravishing Victoria's Secret fragrance all over my bed sheets, turned on the string lights sur-rounding my side of the room for ambiance, and slid into a sexier laced-up cheeky thong as Belle jokingly said, *"We are definitely too close for comfort."*

"What do I do?!" I nervously spoke.

"You take a shot," she said. *"And then another for good luck. You calm down, put on your TV for some background noise, and follow his lead once he enters,"* she said as she made her way over to the door.

"Wait! Don't leave!" I shouted.

"Me staying and watching is a level twelve request, girl," she joked as she closed the door behind her.

I madly paced back-and-forth in my room for the next four and a half minutes until I was interrupted by the buzzing of my phone. Mark was here, and I had to go "sign him in" at the front check-in desk of the residence hall as I looked like a cosplaying prostitute awaiting my police pimp. I ran down the stairs—but not too fast to avoid even *more* sweat droplets from forming—and met him at the desk.

"Mmm, hey hun," he said as he took a swig of his water bottle. He handed over his ID to the staff member, signed his name, and said, *"Yeah, I'll be heading to her room,"* as he winked.

"Room number, please," the staff member said as he rolled his eyes.

"Room 306," I embarrassingly shared knowing that my sexy time was now officially documented.

As we walked past the front desk and turned toward the staircase, Mark asked me if I wanted to "slug back" his drink concoction. Feeling my nerves take over my body, I obliged. We continued to pass over the water bottle until we sucked down the very last droplet. I was already pretty drunk before, but I felt a blackout slowly approaching.

I have to do this fast, I thought to myself as I saw Mark stumble to get into my room. I made my way over to my twin bed as he closed the door. He, too, sat down right next to me. He took the back of his hand and grazed it along the side of my face.

"You're fucking sexy," he said in a playfully frisky manner.

Mark grabbed my face and started kissing me—and damn, he was good at it. He even dragged his callous-filled fingers over my fishnet stockings and would moan as he inched closer to my inner thighs.

"I love your curves," he lustily said as he took his hand from my thigh and finessed his way into my shirt to tease my breasts.

He hands you a drink that he poured or mixed himself.

RATIONALIZING THE RED FLAG: *"We're partying together! You know, just having fun. Plus, we're both nervous as hell, and it eases the nerves."*

WHAT I SHOULD'VE DONE: Declined drinking from his water bottle. (This could've led to a terribly dangerous outcome.)

I FORGIVE MYSELF FOR: Making this sexual encounter more of a priority than having had an amazing mind-blowing connection with someone that could've led to mind-blowing sex... while haphazardly drinking something I didn't know.

IF IT HAPPENS AGAIN: I will not drink to the point of no return to help me feel ready for sex.

SELF-LOVE LESSON: Surrounding myself with people who elevate me and my mindset is more important than surrounding myself with people who just want me for sexual gratification.

After a few moments, he stood up from the bed and aggressively unzipped his pants. A shimmy proceeded as he tried to alleviate this physical barrier from his lower extremities. The sound of his belt buckle smacking the floor while his pants wrapped around his ankles oddly turned me on—but not as much as the imprint of *it* peeking through his gray boxer briefs while it rested in my direct line of vision. He proceeded to rub himself as he bit his lip and locked eyes with me sitting on the edge of my bed.

After teasing me with his own foreplay, he ripped off his briefs and blessed me with his thick ten-inch girthy wonder. (To this day, I feel like I should have won some kind of award for being manhandled by this on my first go-round.)

"You like?" Mark questioned.

"Mhhhhm," I responded as I felt the liquor overtake my body.

Mark then pushed my back into the bed, pried my thong off of my body with his teeth, and spit it out across the room in the hottest pornstar-like manner. He threw my legs up and grazed his tongue all over me and seduced every crevice.

With one swift motion, he then flipped me over and pushed himself into me.

"FUCK!" I half-moaned, half-cried. That first point-of-entry made my entire body cringe with its jolt of pain.

I mentally tried to correlate this pain to getting a new tattoo: the first few needle pricks always sting, but then the body tends to acclimate to the pain and the experience becomes quite bearable (hell, even enjoyable). Except, I was wrong in this instance—the throbbing worsened with each stroke as if my cervix was being scraped. It shockingly disturbed me knowing that I was more than lubricated, too. I bit the pillow in front of me as he continued to pound into me. I kept telling myself to breathe and that it'd be over relatively soon. To speed up the process, I started throwing my back into it more, which created this ripple-like sound effect as I smacked against his legs.

"Daaaaaaamn," he moaned.

It was working.

I knew that once he grabbed my waist with all of his strength and deeply plunged into my backside that it was coming to an end. He literally finished this off by unloading directly into me. His body then fell into mine as he exerted his final force.

"Goddamn, hun," he said in between his panting as he weakly pushed himself up.

I turned myself over and stood up so that I could put on some sweatpants from my drawer.

"You may want to wipe yourself first," he cautioned.

He tries to and/or effectively fucks you without a condom—and without even asking.

RATIONALIZING THE RED FLAG: *"We were just living in the moment and so attracted to one other."*

WHAT I SHOULD'VE DONE: Realized as soon as he got naked that there was no condom and told him that I wouldn't move forward without one.

I FORGIVE MYSELF FOR: Not stopping him.

IF IT HAPPENS AGAIN: I will always use protection (until, of course, we're in a serious relationship and have both been tested).

SELF-LOVE LESSON: I am worthy of being loved and respected as more than a physical object.

I looked down and saw his semen scattered all along my upper thighs—while blood simultaneously trickled down from my genital area. I ferociously flipped through my drawers to find a towel as I tried to mask my internal terror.

"Why are you bleeding like that?!" he questioned.

"You're just… so big," I lied to stroke his ego as I cleaned the muck from my inner thighs. He smiled.

"Let me get that when you're done, hun," he said.

Once I tossed him the towel, he wiped himself up so that he, too, could put his clothes back on. Now dressed, Mark said, *"Goodbye!"* and then made his way out of my door. He didn't even give me a kiss on the cheek.

As the door closed on his shadow, I sank into my bed and cried. I was numb. I couldn't believe that I just gave myself for the very

Looking Within at Personal
RED FLAGS

- You put yourself down.

- You want to lose your virginity without thinking of who you really are losing it to.

- You feel pressured to do things according to societal standards or forced timelines as opposed to the natural progression of your own life (i.e. a "deadline" to lose your virginity).

- You turn to alcohol when you're feeling bad about yourself. (This was a natural theme for me.)

- You have sex with a stranger without any form of contraception.

- You try to curate, control, and force experiences and are not satisfied until it happens according to your timeline.

- You're always looking for romantic permanence in a person. (It's okay to seek out temporary hook-ups and explore your sexuality in all of its uniquely beautiful greatness, but you need to clearly communicate your expectations.)

- You believe that relationships are supposed to start with sexual encounters.

- You solely look at physical attributes when choosing a potential partner.

THE BOY WHO CRIED CHEAT

I'm all about the power of manifestation—especially if someone looks you dead in the eyes and says, *"I am going to cheat on you."* That's an immediate **red flag** on the play, and you should forfeit from that game as I promise you this: you will not come out victorious. Unlike my warning and knowledge now, I decided I would not only play but gamble on the outcomes, too.

Most of this story stems from the premise that I was lonely: my friends during our junior year of college celebrated their twenty-first birthdays and, being that I was the baby of the bunch and needed to wait until October of our senior year, I was alone while they graduated from the house party scene to the bars and clubs. Though I dabbled with the idea of buying a fake ID from this one shady foreign website to join in on the festivities, I refrained as I didn't want to push my luck with the law. After all, I had already been handcuffed to a bench in a police station just one year prior.

It was a wet snow kind of day in early March of my sophomore year. As I was driving home from the mall, I saw a police car slide directly behind me from the left lane. I'm not sure why in that particular moment fear completely overtook my body as my hands gripped the steering wheel and my heart's RPM raced faster than that of my engine. Once the red and blue lights set-off and hypnotized me from my rearview mirror, my entire body soaked in sweat. I pulled over into a hotel's parking lot off of the main road and waited. I knew something was *off* when nearly seven minutes had passed and I hadn't been approached by the officer. Two more police cars then swiftly swooped into the parking lot and completely boxed in my car.

"*Remain in the vehicle and place your hands where we can see them!*" I heard the officer state over his loudspeaker.

I quickly called my one best friend, Kayleigh, and left her the following voicemail message: "*I THINK I'M ABOUT TO GET ARRESTED! WHAT DO I DO?!*" (As if I had any control over the situation.)

The officers approached my car from both sides. "*Please state your name,*" the officer demanded.

"*Brianna McCabe,*" I whimpered as I strangled my steering wheel and motioned my head toward my passenger seat, which had my license, registration, and insurance sprawled across its surface.

"*Ma'am, are you aware that there is a warrant out for your arrest?*" he replied.

"*Excuse me, what?*" I panicked. "*For what?!*"

"*I am going to need you to step out of the vehicle,*" the officer calmly stated.

"*Sir, I have no idea what is going on!*" I started to cry.

"*Ma'am, there's a warrant out for your arrest from having failed to appear in court,*" he said.

"*Me?!*" I now sobbed. "*For what?!*"

"*Ma'am, my system doesn't allow me to look that deeply into it,*" he said. "*I'm going to need to handcuff you, and you're going to have to come with me to the station for processing.*"

"Can... can I at least call my mom and let her know?" I said while now in full hysterics.

"You can at the station," the officer softly shared. *"Listen, I'll just handcuff you in the front and I'll do it loosely so it doesn't hurt, okay?"*

"I just don't understand what I... what I did!" I wept.

While I now sat hunched in the back of the cop car, the officer called his staff over at the station and asked his personnel to "look deeper" into the intricacies of my warrant. Apparently, I was issued a warrant for having failed to appear in court (that I was never notified of) as a result of a parking ticket (that I assume flew off of my car) in my college town.

"Officer, I promise you I have no idea what is going on!" I cried. *"If I had a ticket I would've immediately paid for it!"*

"Ma'am, there is nothing that I can do," he consoled. *"I do know, though, you are going to incur a slew of fees now—even now, you're going to have to be bailed out."*

"BAILED OUT?!" I cried. *"Oh my god, am I a criminal now? Is this when you take my mug shot?"* I cried to the officer as I looked down at my handcuffs.

"Ma'am," he said as he tried not to laugh, *"this is only protocol and you've done nothing criminal."*

"Do I get my one phone call?" I sobbed.

"Yes," he slightly giggled. *"You watch entirely too much television."*

When given the chance, I immediately dialed my mom and shouted, *"Mom! MOM! I need you to come bail me out of jail right now!"*

"HAAAAA, you're funny Bri!" she said as the phone clicked and my call was disconnected.

The complexion drained from my face as I looked over at the officer in dire panic: *"Sir! My mom just hung up. Can you somehow please call her for me, Mr. Officer?!"*

"I mean, I don't really do this, but you do need to get bailed out so that

you don't have to spend the night in a holding cell," he said as he asked me for her 10 digits.

"Ma'am, this is Officer Randy with the Police Department and we're currently holding your daughter until someone can ba—..." he said until he was interrupted.

"WHAAAAAAAAAAT!?" I heard my mom scream through his phone's speaker. I was then able to piece together the following: *"I'm at least... hour away. Uh, uh... let me see... get in touch... friends at school!"*

About thirty minutes later, I was told by Officer Randy that my friends Kayleigh and Anne had paid my $350 bail and were waiting for me at the front of the station. As I was uncuffed from the bench and given back my cell phone, I noticed that my inbox was flooded with hundreds of texts from my friends trying to figure out the reasoning for the arrest.

"We have a bet going on, Bri! You need to answer!" Scarlett's sixth text stated.

"Do you live some kind of secret life we don't know about?" Charlie sarcastically said.

"It's 3 p.m. on a Sunday so this is throwing me off. I'd like to believe that drunk driving isn't a possibility knowing you, so I'm genuinely baffled," Lizzy shared.

When I responded that it was a result of an unpaid parking ticket, Charlie responded that it was "rather anticlimactic." I must admit, though, the #FreeBri hashtag on Twitter was quite comical.

"All of this time wanting to roleplay with handcuffs and you finally got the real deal," Kayleigh laughed as she met me outside of the station. *"Only you..."*

Yes, only me within my friend circle—which is why I didn't want to chance it with a fake ID. That, and between the near-thousand dollars in court fees and fines over the course of that year, my energy and time could be best channeled into a job outside of my on-campus work. I figured that the fastest way to earn money would be to enter the service industry. I basically started my search amongst restaurants whose food I loved: which, to be fair, didn't filter out much.

The first place to call me in for an interview was this sports bar. Though I didn't have experience, the general manager seemed to enjoy my personality and wide-open weekend availability. Being that the restaurant was a chain, the general manager and I came to an agreement that during the school year I would work at this location as a hostess and then, during summer break, transfer over to the location nearest my home. Hopefully, too, by that time I would have advanced my skill set as a hostess and transitioned into waitressing.

Being a hostess and ringing in to-go orders wasn't the fast money that I initially anticipated. Instead, I was collecting minimum wage and sometimes taking home $12 in cash from tips. The monetary void was filled with other perks, though, such as being able to indulge in any food orders that weren't picked up by the customer at the end of the night—which, for the front-of-house staff after a long day of being on our feet, was basically like hitting the lottery. Then there was this bonus of becoming a psychologist after having to quickly immerse yourself into the study of human behavior with constant questions such as:

- What can I do to increase my tip with this customer?

- Which new server will sleep with the seasoned bartender—and why is this environment so horny?

- How can I convince this other worker to pick up my shift next weekend?

- Which server will have a meltdown and walk out on their shift tonight?

- How long do I think this new manager will last?

- Which table will try to get a free meal today?

It really was a dynamic, fast-paced study—and fortunately, I was able to observe this alongside my one best friend to this day, Chelly.

"I never realized the movie Waiting was this spot-on," I laughed to Chelly as we witnessed one of the server's yell at another for "always getting the good party sections."

"They really get so flustered so quickly," she laughed as she stuffed a to-go bag with plastic forks and knives.

"Girl," I said with a pause, *"working over the summer without you is going to suck so bad."*

"Ugh, tell me about it," she said, *"but now you have a new pool of people to watch that you'll have to tell me all about."* She then nudged me in a way that almost solidified a promise that our friendship wouldn't end—and then picked up the ringing phone to jot down a new order.

Although I wasn't granted the opportunity to become a waitress at the restaurant closest to my school, the at-home location was short-staffed and welcomed me as a waitress once the start of summer break commenced. I was informed that I was going to be joining three new servers on my first day, too, which lessened the "awkward blow." My one new manager particularly grew fond of me after I stated that I could work practically every day being that I was only twenty years old and my now-legal friends wanted to enjoy their first beach bar season.

On day one, I quickly scoped out the culture. Though the characters were different, the personalities were oddly similar. You had the handful of creepy cooks who forever looked at you through the expo line with wandering eyes, the one OG cook who would sneak you a free meal at any given time, that one seductress of a bartender who teased every-one (including the staff), the one grumpy night manager who hated his profession, the one chill manager that everyone loved and tried to schmooze, the mature servers who have been in the industry for years and refused to change their ways, the slow-paced but suave bartender who somehow charmed his ways into the beds of several regulars, the

"I think so?" I responded. *"Maybe? I'm not entirely sure. He hasn't really made any moves."*

"Why don't you ask him what's up?" she replied.

"Isn't that a bit too in-your-face and pushy?" I shared.

"Girl, you better use that pussy power you got," she lectured. *"And if he ain't droolin' over you, find someone who will."*

Later that day, I approached Jay by the POS station and told him that the two of us should hang out after work. Though it'd be after midnight, I told him that we could meet-up at this well-lit park near my house and just walk around. After we finished sanitizing our tables, sweeping the floors, refilling the condiments, and cleaning the soda machines, Jay hopped in his car and followed me to the park.

As he stepped out of his car and closed the door, he looked at me and jokingly said, *"This is a weird location and time for a date."*

"But you accepted, so who's the weird one here?" I laughed.

As we walked around the park in our food-stained work outfits and non-slip shoes, I looked over at him and embraced the courage to ask, *"So, what are we doing?"*

"Walking around a park at 1 a.m. like some rebel middle schoolers," he chuckled.

"No, no, I mean like, what exactly are we?" I asked.

He paused both the banter and his walking strides. For nearly twenty seconds, the silence of the darkness surrounding us was nearly deafening.

"Bri, I don't know how to tell you this, but I'm not looking for anything serious right now," he finally let out. *"I'm turning twenty-one in a few weeks, and I know that I'll probably go a little crazy."*

"So you've just been leading me on this whole time?" I questioned.

"It's not that easy," he signed. *"I really, really like you. I just know if I make it official… I am going to cheat on you."*

"Wait, what?" I shockingly responded. *"Are you, like, a habitual cheater? I'm confused why you'd say that?!"*

He tells you his red flag...
and you blatantly ignore it.

RATIONALIZING THE RED FLAG: *"He didn't mean it! Plus, he probably was never with the right woman who made him ever want to truly settle down and be loyal!"*

WHAT I SHOULD'VE DONE: Believed him when he told me.

I FORGIVE MYSELF FOR: Still exploring the relationship.

IF IT HAPPENS AGAIN: I will walk away and accept what he says at face-value as being a red flag that I shouldn't ignore.

SELF-LOVE LESSON: I need to recognize my worth, solidify my self-respect, and establish my boundaries which I will use as a guide to either allow or deny someone access into my life. Because I so deeply yearned for external validation to make me feel "full," I accepted less than the bare minimum just to, well, feel anything at all. Disregarding someone's comment about how they would treat me or go about a potential relationship yet staying because I desperately wanted any form of companionship (whether or not he was faithful, mature, or respectful), shows just how little I valued myself at the time. I must love myself to therefore set the precedent for what I am willing to accept—and being told that it was a guarantee that I'd be cheated on is not on that list.

"I've cheated on my ex before, but I was young and immature," he said. *"Now, I'm just conflicted because I don't want to be tied down, but I do really like you and want to be with you."*

"So now you're older yet still immature? Got it," I snarkily responded. I then mimicked Mimi's statement from earlier by continuing, *"You know what, I want to devote my time to a man who knows what he wants, and not a confused boy."*

"You asked for the truth and now you're mad at the answer?" he laughed. *"Yo, goodnight,"* he added as he turned around and made his way back toward his car.

(In retrospect, this was a semi-healthy moment in comparison to my previous interactions with the landfill of trash that I used to swan dive into and do breast strokes in. After all, he was honest in that he didn't want a relationship, so he did try to back off.)

The next day at work, the animosity between Jay and me was abundantly evident. It didn't help, either, that it was a relatively slow shift, and we couldn't distract ourselves with interactions from guests. When approached by Mimi roughly an hour into the day, I told her about the conversation that ensued after our shift last night.

"Girl, we all told you he was extra and corny," she said.

"Not what I want to hear right now..." I remarked.

"You get hit on all of the time here," she said, *"so what the fuck you want with him?"*

"I don't know," I said. *"I like his soul?"*

"What the FUCK?" she said as she let out the heartiest laugh I've ever provoked. *"You're funny as hell. His soul. Girl, goodbye."*

As our manager started announcing cuts, we were informed that Jay would be among the first round of individuals to leave work and then I could follow suit during the next wave.

Prior to Jay leaving, he approached me and said, *"Hey, about last night..."*

"I really don't want to hear it," I interrupted.

"If you get out at a decent hour, why don't you come over to my house later tonight and let's talk," he suggested. *"I was up all night thinking, and I need to talk to you."*

"I don't really want to have this awkward conversation at your house," I shared.

"I have the place to myself," he said. *"My parents are out of town for*

the week. Come on, Bri, just let me have this conversation with you."

"I'll think about it," I said as I turned and walked away.

Not even an hour later, I was informed by my manager that I, too, could finish up my side work, roll some silverware, and go home. I texted Jay to let him know that I'd be heading home to "handle a few things" (which really meant "take a shower") and that I could be free later that evening.

"Okay great," he responded as he then sent me his address in the immediate next text.

When I parked and walked up the steps to his front door, I couldn't help but notice a grouping of rose petals scattered along the doormat. I knocked on the door and heard Jay shout from the inside, *"Come in!"*

Once I opened the door, a trail of rose petals led me toward the kitchen where Jay was preparing a meal.

"I hope you like chicken francese," he said. *"And save room for dessert,"* he added as he opened the oven door and gave me a peek at his German chocolate cake.

"What… is going on?" I asked.

"Just follow the petals downstairs, and I'll be there in a bit," he responded.

I descended into his basement, which unveiled itself to be his own mini apartment with a living room, bathroom, bedroom, and laundry room. The rose petals led me to the center of his living room as they then jumped from the floor to atop his table in the shape of a heart. He further decorated this tabletop with several lit tealight candles and two glasses of red wine. Several petals were also scattered along his black leather sectional couch. My favorite television show, *South Park*, was already queued up on the television as I heard Cartman's quips in high-definition audio.

A few minutes later, I heard Jay's footsteps waltz down his staircase as linguini danced off of the sides of the two savory lemon dishes he was attempting to balance in his hands. He laid the plates on the table and sat down beside me on the couch.

"Bri, I really am so sorry for what I said yesterday," he said. *"The idea of settling down scares me."*

"I just don't understand the complete 180 that is going on right now," I replied.

"That was stupid of me to say," he said. *"I really do like you… and I'm not sure how a birthday is going to change that."*

"You seemed pretty adamant that you'd cheat on me," I stated.

"I don't know why I said that," he said. *"I would never hurt you like I did my ex."*

Jay disclosed the dynamics of his high school relationship and boiled it down to being "young, dumb, and immature." As he described it, both of them were friends who then acted on pubescent impulses and lazily decided to date in order to solidify a solid sex schedule for two years.

"Both of us cheated," he admitted. *"Now, though, it's abundantly clear what I have in front of me, and I'm not letting it go."*

"I just don't understand how this all changed in less than twenty-four hours," I said.

"I realized how much I missed you," he said as he grabbed a hold of my hand. *"Bri, I want you to be my girlfriend."*

Having never had a boyfriend before, I shockingly absorbed this statement and abruptly responded, *"Wait, really?"*

"Really," he said.

"Okay," I smiled. *"I'll be your girlfriend."*

Without having even touched our food, we made our way into his bedroom where he delicately stripped me of my clothing and pleased me in every possible way. Every now and then he'd moan, *"This is mine now."* Though overly assertive, it turned me on knowing that I was being claimed for the very first time in my life. We later ate dinner, drank wine, and then proceeded with round two as we licked chocolate cake off of each other.

He goes from commitment-phobe to boyfriend within twenty-four hours.

RATIONALIZING THE RED FLAG: *"He was just afraid."*

WHAT I SHOULD'VE DONE: Stayed friends for a long time.

I FORGIVE MYSELF FOR: Judging a connection based on the dynamics of the physical relationship. I could've enjoyed a beautiful dinner and told him I wanted to really get to know him before becoming a girlfriend and going to the bedroom.

IF IT HAPPENS AGAIN: I will allow someone to be honest with me without judgment—and I will be honest right back.

SELF-LOVE LESSON: Commitment is important in a relationship. If someone is fearful about being in a committed relationship, then remain platonic for as long as possible. Fear is normal, but rushing things can be a catalyst for a hot mess.

At the restaurant during our upcoming shifts, Mimi couldn't help but notice our mood shift. *"What happened to y'all now?"* she questioned.

"He realized what he had and decided to ask me to be his girlfriend," I gleefully responded.

"He changed up THAT quickly?" she asked. *"Corny as hell still, but whatever makes you happy."*

I was happy—at least initially, as we continued to have our regularly scheduled date nights. The frequency of our outings were disrupted once he turned twenty-one, though, and he transitioned to going out with his guy group instead. He started to continuously call out of work and leave my messages on "read" for hours while he actively posted videos of himself pouring liquor down the throats of provocatively dressed women straight from the bottle.

"He looks like a fuckboy," Lizzy snarled as she tapped through his

Snapchat stories from my phone.

"He swears up and down that it's just for show and to impress his friends," I replied.

"He doesn't respect you," she said. *"Have you ever been on his Snapchat?"*

"Well, no, but he…" I managed to say.

"Is hiding you? Yes, exactly," she interjected. *"He wanted his lame-ass German chocolate cake and to eat it, too. Girl, he needs to go."*

Jay insisted that his lack of posting me wasn't a result of "hiding me," rather it was out of habit of having never posted a woman he's dated before.

"It's just not something I'm used to," he explained. *"But I can try and work on it, I guess."*

By "work on it," Jay really meant that I would grace his Snapchat stories—which disappeared after twenty-four hours—only a handful of times throughout the duration of our entire relationship. In those few instances, though, I will admit that I finally felt desirable. However, those feelings fleeted shortly after the story expired.

As I prepared to move into my new dorm for the start of my senior year, I feared physically separating from Jay. Although I invited him to visit the first few weekends and finally meet my friends, he declined my offer so that he could "figure out his life." His place of mindful meditation and deep thoughtfulness must've been the local clubs based on his constant flurry of social media posts in those atmospheres.

"I think I'm going to start going home on the weekends to hang with Jay," I suggested to Kayleigh as I zoomed in on Jay's new Instagram pictures to hopefully alleviate any unwarranted suspicions of him cheating.

"It's your senior year, and you're about to finally turn twenty-one," she insisted. *"Why would you do that?"*

"I don't know…" I shrugged. *"I just miss him."*

"Well it doesn't appear that he misses you," she commented. *"But I support you either way, always."*

I spent the weekend of my twenty-first birthday and every weekend thereafter traveling back home to spend time with Jay. While I deeply saddened my friends by practically disappearing, they did understand my clinginess as a result of this being my first relationship. They may not have supported my choice in a partner, but they supported any decisions that brought me inner happiness—even if it was only temporary. Their general understanding shifted to tough love quickly, though, as I started to voice concerns of certain behaviors "just not feeling right."

"Every single time that we're together, Jay turns his phone face-down and refrains from answering any texts while I sit directly next to him," I shared with my friends as we drank coffee in-between our classes. *"He claims it's because he wants to 'live in the moment.'"*

"That's super sketchy," Scarlett warned.

"And I can't lie, one time I peeked, and I saw it was a text from his ex," I admitted.

"Well, did you look?" Kayleigh questioned.

"Ugh, I did," I disclosed. *"They were sending each other funny memes and pictures with subtle but not over-the-top flirting."*

"What exactly do you mean?" Belle pushed.

"Like, there were a few tongue face exchanges," I said.

"I really hope he's not playing with you or we're going to have to step in somehow," Scarlett said as she aggressively threw a fake-punch into the air.

"If he's such a party animal, I just don't understand why he refuses to come out here with you and the rest of us," Kayleigh chimed in. *"I don't want to be negative, but I just don't know what else to think."*

Both my gut and mind knew that my friends were more than likely accurate in their judgements, but my heart didn't necessarily want to believe that someone could be proactively causing me pain. I thought about their statements all day, though, to the point where I couldn't not bring this up during our phone call later that night.

He turns his phone face down whenever he's with you.

RATIONALIZING THE RED FLAG: *"He wants to be completely and totally focused on me without distraction."*

WHAT I SHOULD'VE DONE: Called him out on his texts and his Snapchat. There's no reason to want to look like a player if you are in a truly committed relationship.

I FORGIVE MYSELF FOR: Being clingy and not demanding that I be the only woman he should be pouring liquor into.

IF IT HAPPENS AGAIN: I will break up the relationship. I deserve respect.

SELF-LOVE LESSON: Guys can't have their cake and eat it, too. I was allowing this man to do that because I wanted so desperately to be in a relationship.

When I asked his reasoning for avoiding any visits to my college, he responded, *"Seeing you there intimidates and depresses me, Bri. It's a sad reminder of my lost time and progress, really, and how significantly behind I am from getting my degree."*

Hearing the frustration in his voice, I decided to spend the next two weeks crafting a well-organized binder of nearly one dozen potential in- and out-of-state business schools that he could apply to based on his short- and long-term goals. I categorized the schools based on transfer requirements, essay topics, credit costs, location, program rankings, and on-campus amenities. Though my college librarian wasn't happy that I practically murdered a tree in the process of printing these hundreds of pages, I was motivated by the ability to help Jay make the next step in his academic career.

I gifted Jay the binder toward the end of October, which impressed both him and his mom in terms of my dedication to his advancement. For about one week, though, Jay let the binder accumulate dust in the corner of his room as he continued to conduct his own research at the clubs. After a nudge from his mom, though, he finally cracked open the binder and started reading through some of the information that I gathered. Although there were eight in-state universities highlighted, Jay decided that the top school he wanted to attend was the one that was six hours away in Pittsburgh.

"That's not even the best school for exercise science out of the bunch," Jay's mom said.

"But it's more about the experience of living on my own," he shared.

"You know you can do that in-state, right?" his mom questioned as she glanced at me from across the dining room table.

"It's not the same, mom!" he said as he stormed downstairs into his mancave.

"What was that about?" his mom questioned me. *"Boy has some nerve talking to me like that."*

As I walked downstairs, I found Jay feverishly typing away on his laptop.

"What are you doing?" I questioned.

"I'm applying to this school and no one can tell me otherwise!" he snapped.

I sat in silence for the next hour as he slammed the tips of his fingers into his keyboard and populated words on a blank Word document in response to the college essay's topic of overcoming obstacles. When I finally glanced over his shoulder and noticed that his thoughts were scattered and there were no fully cohesive sentences, I offered my help.

"I was hoping you would finally step in!" he barked.

"Whoa!" I said. *"What's with the attitude? I did all of this research FOR YOU, and now you're going to demand my help in writing YOUR essay?"*

"Either help me or go home!" he snapped as he tossed his laptop toward my thighs.

with scenes of themed parties, during my visit he tucked his phone away in his pants pockets to "live in the moment." This minimal action oddly showed his appreciation for me (in a twisted way) after I had driven nearly four hundred miles one-way through hazardous blizzard-like conditions just to see him. The two of us then stayed huddled in his dorm together as we watched television and ordered food deliveries. To mimic Jay, I, too, dismissed the FOMO-inducing Snapchats from my friends back home to feel present.

Practically every weekend thereafter I would trek the twelve hour-loop to his college and back just to see him while I came bearing gifts of liquor, food, and beer pong balls.

"You are way too good to him," Dave once said to me in passing as Jay was using the bathroom.

"Aw thanks!" I blushed in response to the perceived compliment. *"But wait... why am I too good?"* I quickly added.

"You're just a really good person..." he said. As he noticed the bathroom door slowly swing open, he then shifted the topic of conversation to the movie Jay and I were watching.

Despite his roommate's cryptic message, over the next two months I proceeded with my weekly road trips. My already-dingy car further deteriorated in that my tires would catch flats, my battery would completely clunk out, and my engine would sometimes overheat while I'd be stranded on a side road for hours in the middle of the night. I became best friends with the AAA dispatchers as I constantly requested tows and battery jumps—but our relationships then shifted toward frenemies once I was informed that I reached my maximum number of available services and needed to pay for an extension in coverage.

On one instance, while I waited in my car for a roadside assistance driver, I naturally took to social media to pass some time. I happened to look at Jay's Snapchat and view his most recent shirtless mirror selfie where, in the reflection, I noticed that the picture frame I had gifted him and placed on his desk was now face down atop its surface.

"Hey babe, why is our picture frame hidden?" I sadly inquired.

"You're overreacting, Brianna! I just dusted my desk, and it must've fallen. Stop looking into fucking everything and acting crazy!" he responded after thirty minutes.

"I was just wondering, Jay! It looked suspicious. I'm sorry," I replied.

"Don't even bother coming if you're going to bring that fucking attitude and skepticism!" he added.

"Jay, I only have an hour left to go… I'm just waiting for a new tire," I said.

"Seriously change your tone or turn back around," he said.

"I'm sorry, Jay," I replied.

Though I arrived at a later-than-normal time, the weekend routine proceeded as scheduled: we hibernated between his twin-size bed sheets while munching on Cheez-Its. Though I enjoyed the quality time, I grew skeptical of this isolation.

"Hey, babe," I softly said, *"do you think maybe we could switch it up this weekend and finally hang with some of your friends?"*

"You know that I like to relax on the weekends with you," he said. *"Do you not appreciate this quality time alone?"*

"No, no, I do!" I said.

"It doesn't seem like it, Bri!" he snapped. *"I told you that I wouldn't tolerate any questioning this weekend, yet here you are."*

I finally recognized that he had just manipulated the conversation to now be in complete control, yet despite this knowledge, I felt powerless. Internally, I started to harp on each questionable moment that I had experienced in this relationship and repeatedly watched these snippets replay in my mind. Suffocated by his negative behaviors, I fixated on this idea that Jay, a man who claimed to love me, may actually be disrespecting me as a woman.

My friends were right all along, I thought to myself. *But how will I* blank white walls and listened to the rhythmic beeps of my heart rate monitor. *Jay can't just leave me like this.*

After recovering in the hospital and slowly reintegrating back into my daily routine, Jay texted me: *"Bri, we need to talk. I am so sorry that I wronged you like that. I miss you, and I love you."*

The willpower to leave him on "read" as he had done to me on so many nights was ineffective in this situation. Physically and emotionally weak, I crawled back through a slow deployment of text messages describing my prevalent pain.

"I promise to make this up to you," he begged. *"I fucked up."*

"It's my senior year, and you RUINED it!" I said as I practically handed over my power to him. *"I refuse to let you ruin my last few weeks of my senior year."*

"I won't do that, Bri," he said. *"I won't ever hurt you again if you give me the chance.*

Internally, I contemplated whether or not Jay actually loved me. *If he didn't love me, why would he be begging for me back?* I foolishly thought to myself.

Despite the hesitation to engage in further conversation, I allowed Jay the opportunity to reestablish his trustworthiness and replenish my emotionally depleted self. He said that he would drive home the remaining few weekends of the semester to spend time with me, write me love letters, cut off complete interaction from Kayla, leave his phone face up in my presence, and take me on the dates I desperately yearned to go on. Although hesitant and recognizing that this may never progress into romance ever again, I gave Jay a second chance while I myself kept these brief interactions hidden from my loved ones out of embarrassment and shame.

I didn't realize just how deep the hurt ran until we tried to get intimate for the first time since the incident. As he undressed me and tried to enter my now-exposed body, I immediately clammed up and cried knowing that this action wasn't pure to just us anymore. We were infiltrated by infidelity.

"I… I can't do this right now," I bawled.

"Bri, what's wrong?" he asked as he rubbed himself.

"I just can't get over the fact that you were fucking someone else when you were supposed to be with me," I cried.

"I'm sorry," he said. "I guess, uh, I'll just wait until whenever you're ready."

I decided to make him wait for sex until I graduated from college. This way, I could better navigate my feelings, seek clarity without the convoluted nature of orgasms, and carve out the groundwork for my professional career. Once I solidified my first full-time job and received the notification that I was eligible for graduation, I felt ready to potentially give Jay more effort if, of course, it was warranted.

Leading up to my graduation, Jay promised to celebrate my accolades in the most romantic of ways while he continued to shower me in gifts, quality time, and love notes that even Shakespeare himself would've been envious of. Through his actions, I actually started to believe that he felt remorse for his behaviors.

"Bri, I want you to be mine again," Jay said.

"I do miss us," I replied, "but it's hard because this, all of this, is a secret. No one knows I've even been talking to you after what you've done."

"I'm willing to fight for their forgiveness just like I've been fighting for yours," he shared.

"Maybe you can prove it at my graduation party," I said. "After all, everyone will be there."

"Okay, I will," he promised. "But Bri, I really want you to be my girlfriend again. We can keep it a secret until you're ready, babe."

"I don't know, Jay," I said. "I love you, but—"

"Be my girlfriend," he said. "I love you with everything in me… and I fucked up, I know. I'll never do anything like that again, ever."

"Okay, I'll be your girlfriend," I agreed. "I do love you. Otherwise, I *wouldn't be here right now."*

When I informed my closest friends that Jay and I were "trying to make things work again" and that he'd be present at my graduation party, I was practically verbally assaulted in the group chat. I begged my friends to be on their best behaviors while embracing my decision to proceed forward with this relationship. I thought this would be relatively easy for them to implement—except I didn't factor into the equation that liquor that would be ravenously consumed in amounts I haven't quite seen since my freshman year of college.

I was impressed by the caliber of fake niceness that my friends exhibited toward Jay for the first few hours of the party. The event ran smoothly until Lizzy drunkenly—and hilariously (being that confrontation is not in her nature)—muttered under her breath that Jay was a "whore." Now feeling targeted, Jay decided to isolate himself until everyone exited the party. Sadness overcame me as my empathetic nature tried to internally justify that people deserve second chances. So, as you can imagine, I felt rather blindsided when later that night I opened up my presents and noticed that Jay had only gifted me a Hallmark card with a scribbled note on the inside that stated, *"I owe you. Love u, Jay."*

"What's with the note?" I said to Jay as my eyes welled up. *"You owe me? That's all you could write?"*

"Graduation is a sore subject," he said. *"I feel behind in life and like a loser. I don't know."*

"I feel like you said all of these things just to get me back," I cried. *"You could've just written me something a bit more special."*

"Oh, so now you're not appreciative?" he snapped. *"I spent all night with your fake ass friends pretending I liked them FOR YOU, and this is what I get?"* he added as he then left my house and refrained from texting me for the remainder of the night.

All of these promises reached their expiration date once Jay knew that he had me once again. The love notes stopped, the quality time ceased to exist, the openness dissipated, and the sneakiness returned. I didn't realize the extent of his conniving ways until I happened to scroll through Instagram while on my lunch break and stumbled upon Jay's new selfie that he had just posted. Within seconds, Kayla had literally returned into the picture as she commented "BABE!" alongside some heart eye emojis.

My mouth dropped, as did my phone.

As I picked up my phone from the floor and refreshed the page to see who else had commented, I noticed that the comment had disappeared.

I frantically texted Jay: *"I thought you told me that you completely cut Kayla off?"*

"What are you talking about?" he replied.

"I just saw Kayla comment on your photo, and now it's gone," I said after having recognized that he had deleted it out of secrecy. *"You promised me that you'd block her from everything, too."*

"You're fucking nuts and imagining things, bro," he said. *"Go back to work and stop bothering me."* (Hey Pornhub, it's me. Yeah, I'm getting FUCKED again.)

Those words triggered me into a state of anger like I have never experienced. Though I was only a few weeks into my job, I told my boss that I "had an emergency back home to deal with," sprinted to my car, and slammed my foot into the gas pedal as I raced up the highway toward his house at speeds I honestly didn't know my car could handle. I maniacally called Jay, but he kept hitting the "reject" button. I then called Graham and screamed that I was *"GOING TO KILL HIM!"*

"Bri, you need to calm down," he soothingly said. *"I understand you feel betrayed, but you need to go home."*

"FUCK THAT!" I yelled as I continued to drive with my tear-filled vision. *"I'M DRIVING TO HIS HOUSE AND I'M GOING TO KICK HIS ASS!"*

"What are you actually thinking you're going to do?" Graham asked.

"I have a baseball bat in my trunk from my softball league, and I'm going to CRUSH his head against it!" I shouted.

"Bri, LISTEN to me!" he demanded. *"You need to go hom—"* he managed to say before I ended the phone call.

Determined to physically cause Jay pain to reciprocate the invisible wounds he had caused my heart and mind, I found my way at his house within thirty-seven minutes after having shaved off twenty-three from my NASCAR-level driving skills. I busted my car onto his street and haphazardly parked behind one of his neighbor's cars. I then hopped out of the car, sprinted towards his house, and maniacally started pounding my fists against his garage door.

"JAY GET THE FUCK OUT HERE!" I yelled as I squeezed my baseball bat in between my elbow to prevent it from falling in between each thrash.

I then remembered that I knew the code to get into his garage—so I aggressively punched that in and entered into his garage to then break down the final barrier between me and his mancave.

"OPEN THIS FUCKING DOOR!" I screamed in between tears. I took my bat and started whacking away at some of Jay's items such as his shoe rack and workout equipment in the hopes of evoking a reaction. *"JAY, OPEN THIS FUCKING DOOR NOW!"*

After several minutes of mayhem, I exited his garage and decided that I needed to lure him outside. I hid in a bush just on the outskirts of his driveway and pretended to have caused damage to his car by sending him the following text: *"Good luck driving tomorrow."* As I waited for five minutes in the hopes that he'd open the door, my phone buzzed from an incoming call from Graham.

"Bri, where the FUCK are you?" he questioned.

"Graham, I'm going to fucking KILL him!" I angrily whispered.

"You need to leave before he or his parents call the police," he said. *"You've technically already committed the crime of breaking-and-entering."*

"I don't give a FUCK!" I said.

"You worked too damn hard to throw it away for this scumbag," he said. *"Get in your car NOW and go home."*

To avoid being handcuffed in the back of a cop car for the second time in my life, I granted Graham's voice the ability to soothe me into a calmer disposition as he guided me home. Through our conversation, I realized that on the rare occasions that I do feel the essence of true anger, my wrath can be as dangerous as a Category 5 hurricane. This inner fire is fueled by an accumulation of feeling constantly disrespected and stepped on—although I, myself, permitted this violation of my boundaries due to a lack of self-worth.

"You were playing an angry one-sided game of hide-and-go-seek," Graham tried to joke later that night. *"But really, Bri, you need to stop allowing people to constantly cross you."*

"Allllllriiiiight, alright," I responded. *"I know, but damn, at this point I would've rather gone to jail than be lectured by my best friend all night."*

Looking Within at Personal
RED FLAGS

- You want (and expect) the relationship to move incredibly fast.

- You don't heed his warnings about cheating.

- You dive in headfirst to the title "girlfriend."

- You feel worthy when someone "shows you off" on social media. (It makes you feel as if you can finally feel a sense of pride since someone has now "claimed" you.)

- You don't listen to the opinions of your loved ones when it comes to your choices of partners.

- You find yourself apologizing in times that you actually shouldn't.

- You lie to your partner to try and catch him in a lie.

- You go through your partner's phone. (If you feel the need to snoop, is this really a relationship that you should pursue? Relationships should be built on trust and respect... and this right here is the exact opposite.)

- You allow someone to walk all over you to the point of finally "snapping" and exploding—while even potentially getting violently aggressive.

- You literally break-and-enter into someone's house. (Yes, I just personally attacked myself here.)

7

THE NOT-SO-
SERENDIPITOUS
SOULMATE

I never thought that the premise of *90 Day Fiancé* could ever potentially apply to my life, but never say never, right? To preface this part of my life, when I graduated from college, my mom gave me the choice to celebrate my accomplishment in one of two of the following ways:

- Throw a massive banger to which all of my friends and loved ones would be invited.

- Hop on a plane and travel to a country of my choosing (within financial limitations, of course) for a mother-daughter trip.

I knew that I would attend several dozen graduation parties where I would see people I cherished, so I decided to dust off the hand-me-down suitcase and tell my mom that I wanted to visit my ancestral land of Ireland.

So, we got to work—well, okay, *really* my mom did. She connected with a family friend who worked at a travel agency and mapped out our experience so that we could see more than just Dublin. My contribution was basically just scheduling my passport photo. (I wish someone had warned me that I couldn't leave my hair in a messy gym bun. Forced to unravel the sweaty curls by the grouch behind the camera, I ended up with a mugshot similar to what you'd imagine in one of the cast members in *Orange is the New Black* would take.)

I've heard stories about the absolute magnificence of this country's beauty in just the landscape alone, but not a single person I spoke to was able to articulate the breathtaking shades of green that simply draped across its countryside. (I honestly think Benjamin Moore would fail in trying to replicate these pops of pigments.) The second I stepped off of the airplane, I felt this innate connection. Maybe I was getting sentimental knowing that I had roots in terms of my lineage, but my soul felt like it was *home*. This feeling solidified with every single person we met along our journey from Dublin to County Cork and even Galway. The place that solidified my belonging, though, was Killarney. It was in this town that I felt the heart of Ireland pulsate within my very own veins.

The merriest of people seemed to call this quaint area home. Granted, many of them were quite giddy from drinking Guinness (seriously, they would drink stout for breakfast), but they all seemed so genuinely happy. They had a simple way of living, too. It was a culture shock from my materialistically driven lifestyle back in the States. Here, it was all about community and inner peace. Walking into a local pub felt like you were on the set of *Cheers* because, really, everybody knew your name—and if they didn't, they would welcome you into their family with a simple clanking together of your pint glasses. Despite the massive alcohol consumption, it was also to my surprise that I did not witness one single bar fight or altercation (again, very much unlike home).

Our first night in Killarney, mom and I decided to dive into the nightlife scene and watch a local band. After slugging back a few brews, I stumbled into what would become two lifelong friends, Kieran and Finn.

"I'm staaaaaaaarving," I slurred. *"Do you have any munchie food around here?"*

"Yes, Sheila!" a random lad replied back along with some laughter and heavily sped up words I couldn't quite understand. (They talk incredibly fast out there.) *"It seems you're having great craic!"*

"Crack?" I questioned. *"No, no I don't do drugs like that!"*

"No, girl, craic!" he managed to say in between hefty cackles. *"It means great fun, girl!"* he shouted above the band's music as he tapped his pint glass against mine.

"My name is Brianna, by the way!" I exclaimed. *"Do I look like a Sheila or something?"*

"Sheila is a lovely little term for girl!" he replied. *"But it's a pleasure. I'm Kieran!"*

"Sláinte!" Kieran's friend Finn shouted over from his nearby barstool as he raised his mug.

"That basically means cheers or to good health!" Kieran explained.

We danced and sang to the music all night in the most lighthearted of fashions. As Kieran explained, it was pure *craic*. After closing the pub down until the wee hours of the morning, the four of us walked (well, I wobbled) over to a late-night fried chicken sandwich shack and ordered food to-go as we laughed over our accents, the country's not-so-flavorful food (though I loved Ireland, I teased their cuisine for requiring hot sauce and more seasoning), and different lifestyles. The gentlemen walked us back to our hotel just to make sure we didn't get lost—and then we exchanged Facebook and WhatsApp information so that we could pick their brains for more activities to partake in during our stay.

The next morning I woke up to several messages outlining the best local pubs, shops, and "must-see" attractions along the Ring of Kerry, which is a famous driving loop for tourists, along with a *"See you tonight for more craic?"* message from Kieran. My mom, on the other hand, woke up to random, frantic messages from my stepdad accusing her of cheating. I didn't realize this until moments later when he texted me asking me to "be honest" about my mom's "behavior."

"It's my GRADUATION present! What are you talking about?!?!?" I vigorously texted back.

"You're right, I'm sorry," he said. *"Please don't tell mom."*

Yeah, okay, I thought to myself as I rolled my eyes and asked my mom what this was all about...

In retrospect, it was probably his guilty conscience. Not even one year later, my mom discovered that he was cheating on her with one of his old high school flings. My stepdad, not being the most technologically literate of individuals, left his Facebook profile open on our family room's computer. Persistent dinging of chat notifications kept disrupting my mom from her soap opera consumption, so she left the couch to go log out of whoever's account that was. To her dismay, she saw a small chat box in the lower right hand corner pop up on my stepdad's homepage from a woman named Jan calling him "hun" and "baby." Apparently, as my mom told me years later, she spent that entire day scrolling through hundreds of thousands of messages that spanned almost half of a decade. My mom then practically trailed my stepdad's every move for months from that point forward—even recruiting some friends along the way. (Now you probably see where I get it from.)

My mom was determined to "catch him in the act," which she ultimately did. Although she has a tough exterior and doesn't show emotions as freely as I do, I can't even fathom the gut-wrenching pain that my mom felt during this period of her life after having been was deeply in love with this man for years (and I know for a while that he felt the same.) I certainly tried to stay out of their relationship, but I do know that at one point they tried counseling—except, like the Ottomans, their empire (or whatever you want to call it) crumbled, too. Eventually, though, they formally separated and created a casual, respectable adult friendship.

Anyway, my mom didn't let those fleets of texts from my stepdad ruin our vacation. We spent the day not only adventuring but admiring—and we couldn't wait to later reunite with our newfound friends. In pure Irish fashion, we met up at a local pub, dove into some shepherd's pie, and then washed it down with a Bulmers (globally known as Magners). Every single person sitting at the bar then bought my mom and me multiple rounds of drinks to welcome us Americans into their great country. Needless to say, I got drunk in a relatively short period of time—and the night was only just beginning.

I didn't leave the barstool for nearly two hours. After having slurped several ciders, the need to "break the seal" abruptly consumed my thoughts. I fuzzily tried to find the sign to "the jacks" (restroom) so that it could guide me in the right direction—almost as if it was the North Star. On my way out from the ladies room, I haphazardly opened my squinty eyes just enough to realize that the pub was packed. (Clearly, I was living in my own blitzed bubble.) With my eyes latched onto my barstool that Finn was so graciously saving for me, I didn't realize that a lad was making his way toward me from the opposite side of the bar.

"Excuse me, girl, but you are so beautiful," the stranger said as he interrupted my travels. *"Do you fancy a drink?"*

"Oh, thank you!" I bashfully replied. *"I'm good on the drinks, but thank you so much!"*

"Just one," he kindly urged. *"Oh, and my name is Conor!"*

He escorted me over to his little side table and we chatted until the pub closed. Physically, he appeared to be in his mid-twenties and was slightly taller than me, semi-athletic in build, and one of the best dressed of the bunch in the pub. His reddish brown hair seemed to accentuate his nearly transparent freckles that only glistened when the golden light from the pendant fixtures over the bar counter skimmed his face at the proper angle. In conversation, he brought up the fact that he held a degree in mathematics, his family owned one of the staple shoe shops in the area, and he worked in the accounting department at Amazon. We exchanged stories as "just one" drink turned into four or five more. Every so often, Kieran would walk over to check in on me. Being that Killarney is a small town, both Kieran and Conor were very familiar with one another—and I seemed to sense that Kieran wasn't his biggest fan.

Once the night seemed to wind down and the bartenders asked us to leave, Conor walked me outside and insisted that we exchange social media information. As I was squinting down at my phone while leaning against a brick wall for balance, Conor maneuvered his body up against mine.

"Can I please give you a proper kiss goodbye?" he asked as the crescent moon reflected off of his pupils.

"No, no!" I replied as I wiggled my way out from his hold. *"I have a boyfriend!"* (At the time, I was still dating Jay.)

"He wouldn't have to know!" he awkwardly laughed. *"It could be our little secret."*

Now I know why Kieran was clearly not a fan of his character. *"No, I'm good,"* I said as I walked toward my mom, Kieran and Finn.

"I was only kidding, love!" he shouted in the distance.

Once I made my way back, Kieran laughed and told me that he was trying to give me "the eyes" throughout the night to leave my conversation with Conor.

He doesn't accept your boundaries.

RATIONALIZING THE RED FLAG: *"We were drinking."*

WHAT I SHOULD'VE DONE: Given him a firmer "back off" and never talked to him again.

I FORGIVE MYSELF FOR: Being a fairly sloppy drunk.

IF IT HAPPENS AGAIN: I will have a game plan with whoever I am with at the bar about drinking and talking to strangers.

SELF-LOVE LESSON: Occasionally partying is okay, but if I feel the need to drink too much I will recognize what I am really looking for instead. Loving myself means honoring my body, too.

"There's just something about that guy..." Kieran murmured. *"But let's face it, ye are some of the best looking girls we've seen around these parts in quite some time!"* he jokingly said. *"He probably was smitten by your beauty, you see!"*

Once our friends got us back safe and sound, we promised once more to meet the next day to celebrate our last night in Killarney. I opened the door to our hotel room, waltzed over to the bed, and let my body dissolve into the bed sheets. I woke up the next morning still wearing the clothes from the night prior—including my beanie, jacket, and boots.

"Wow, Bri, you clearly can't hang," my mom joked as she greeted me awake with a fresh cup of coffee.

My bargaining for "just five more minutes of sleep" didn't work— which I now can appreciate given that we had less than twenty-four hours in Killarney before we made our way to Dublin to head back home. I checked my phone and saw that I received several texts from

Kieran with more sightseeing stops and a few from Conor apologizing for his persistently flirty behavior.

That day, mom and I drove around and explored more of the country—taking in the greenery, people, and cultural values. I jokingly said that I wanted to reach out to Yankee Candle's development team and somehow have them capture the essence of Killarney in a glass jar so that I could regularly light it and symbolically travel back to these memories as the flame danced its own Irish jig around the wick.

That last night in Killarney I don't remember much—Kieran and Finn basically shoved my mouth under the nozzle of a beer tap and told me to keep drinking. (Okay, that didn't *really* happen, but the drinks did not stop flowing, and I never had an empty pint glass.) It was a grand ol' time of hugs, chugs, and pure *craic*. At one point, the four of us made our way to our hotel's bar that had a piano situated right near the front of the lobby. One of the guests serenaded us with the most beautiful Gaelic song that, in English, translated to a message of *"This isn't a goodbye, but a see you later."* I started hysterically crying at the thought of leaving my new friends and potentially never seeing them again.

"It will be okay," Kieran comforted me. *"I promise this isn't the end."*

"Girl, don't cry!" Finn echoed.

"I love you guys and this place so much," I managed to make out in between sniffles as my mom recorded my wreck-of-a-self on her phone in the name of "memories" (thanks, ma). *"I've never felt this way before."*

"That's because ye have never had Guinness from Ireland before in this amount, my dear!" Kieran wittily responded.

I hugged the two of them so hard with the fullest intentions of never letting go—that was until my mom checked the time and realized that we only had three measly hours left to get some rest, pack our bags, and hop in a scheduled car ride to Dublin. We hugged once more and separated. The second that I entered our hotel room, I once again fell asleep fully clothed.

I basically vomited the entire next day en route to Dublin—and I was barely even conscious enough to make my way to and through the airport. I looked like Bambi trying to learn how to walk while also attempting to roll my carry-on suitcase and keep a garbage can within a four-second sprint. I swore I'd never drink again. (That's laughable.) When I was semi-alert enough to check my phone, I saw several text messages from Kieran and Finn wishing me safe travels along with a text from Conor: *"I am so very sorry for overstepping a boundary. You must forgive me. Please. Get home safe, Bri."*

I accepted this stranger's apologies and allowed him to remain my Facebook and WhatsApp friend for years to follow—which somehow landed me back in Ireland for St. Patrick's Day a few years later. (Sorry in advance, mom.)

He finds you from 3,000 miles away after he breaks a boundary and begins to charm you.

RATIONALIZING THE RED FLAG: *"Everyone makes mistakes when they drink too much, right?"*

WHAT I SHOULD'VE DONE: Not accepted his social media requests and closed the chapter on that lad from Ireland.

I FORGIVE MYSELF FOR: Being overly forgiving.

IF IT HAPPENS AGAIN: I will stay true to the boundaries I set and remember why I set them.

SELF-LOVE LESSON: Breaking boundaries is a violation of trust while setting and upholding boundaries is an act of self-love. I can forgive others without allowing them back into my life—especially in a romantic way.

It's funny how a "like" or "poke" on Facebook could really make something out of nothing. What started out as a few back-and-forth internet gestures slowly transitioned into occasional *"Hey what's up?"* chats. It picked up in terms of conversation, though, after I watched *P.S. I Love You* and mentioned to Conor how much I missed the beauty that was his country. He jokingly told me that I could come visit, but that would be absurd... right? And so we talked—almost daily despite the time difference—for several weeks. At first it was more along the lines of a friendly pen pal, but then he'd subtly get flirty. In fact, we'd plan to watch the same movies on the same nights and recap the movie in sync. He'd refer to them as long-distance date nights.

As the weeks progressed, he'd start calling me via WhatsApp. Our conversations would span anywhere in length from a few minutes to well over two hours. It was during one of these blush-filled banters that he introduced the idea of potentially applying for a work visa and relocating to my home state through his company, which had offices only one hour away from me.

"This almost feels serendipitous," he softly said.

"Well that's a fancy choice of a word," I giggled back to Conor.

"Wait, have you never seen the movie Serendipity?" he questioned.

"No, I don't believe I have," I replied. *"If it isn't an Adam Sandler or Will Smith movie, I probably haven't seen it."*

"Well that's your job for tonight," he said.

A quick Google search summarized the plotline: it's about these two people who were so wildly connected at first sight that they were convinced they'd end up together one day. Now, in my mind I tried to think back to what it felt like the first night we met. I was drunk, but I do recall thinking that he was a good looking fellow (and I didn't think it was the beer goggles). However, I didn't "put myself out there" as I was in a relationship at the time (though now I was single). Being that he just planted this seed of there having been a connection, though, I naively agreed and started to wholeheartedly believe in that narrative myself. And so I watched his movie recommendation—and swooned at the romantic gesture. That night, Conor asked me if he could have my home address to mail me a surprise. A few weeks later, *Love in the Time of Cholera*, a novel by Gabriel García Márquez (which was a focal point to the plotline in *Serendipity*), was delivered along with a note that said: *"To being serendipitous."* He was speaking my love language.

Determined to somehow see Conor once again in person (and not be restricted to the confines of WhatsApp messages), I asked his thoughts on potentially meeting in Ireland for St. Patrick's Day. At first, I don't think that he believed I would actually follow the Nike slogan and *Just Do It*.

"You're funny, girl," he messaged.

"Flights are only around $450 round trip," I replied. *"I will seriously book it right now, and I'll fly out exactly three weeks from today."*

"You are determined," he laughed. *"I'll chat with my boss once he gets back from his break."*

Not even one hour later, Conor was approved to take the week off. Not even five minutes after that message was opened on my end, a plane ticket was booked. Where I was going to stay, how I was going to travel, and what I was going to do was still in question, but I somehow trusted that it would miraculously work itself out. (As a nod to the movie *Little Nicky*, I just believed in the butterflies.) I texted a confirmation code of my ticket to my best friend, Luella, who then immediately called me.

"Brianna, are you out of your mind?" Luella questioned.

"What?!" I responded. *"It'll be an adventure!"*

"Girl, you're going to a country all alone with an absolute stranger," she said. *"You need to listen to me and like, either cancel that ticket or... or... I'm coming with you!"*

"Luella, what if this is my person?" I said. *"I need to go."*

"Alright I guess we're going with option two!" she laughed. *"Girl, not*

everything is a fairytale… Jeez, what's the flight number?"

"*Thanks? I love you, too,"* I awkwardly joked.

Luella, my little Libra twin, has the most quirky and appealing charm. Like a cherry on top of any good sundae, she is always dressed in some kind of statement fashion hat (that no one else could effectively pull off quite like her). Then there's her energy, which allures and hypnotizes nearly everyone within a thirty-foot radius of her presence. She's just this rare, unique, and creative breed that is captivating. Whereas I'd consider myself relatively crafty with a writing tool, I am unmatched by Luella who can turn any object or surface into a canvas and create utter beauty. And her zest for adventure and spontaneity? It's unlike anything I've ever seen. (She actually inspired me to get my first impromptu tattoo, which is a Friday the 13th tattoo that we have permanently and identically inked together on our ankles.) She's this sweet, yet brutally-honest-when-necessary, soul that I am blessed to call one of my best friends.

"*Hey, Conor,"* I texted him. "*I hope you don't mind, but my best friend Luella is coming, too."*

"*Oh?"* he typed back. "*I mean, I guess that's okay. Ye are welcome to stay at my place. I'm a bit of a neat freak so ye don't have to worry!"*

"*Are you sure?"* I confirmed. "*We don't want to be a burden… we can figure it out."*

"*My house is right in the heart of Dublin, my dear, it's fine!"* he said. "*I can get ye from the airport, too."*

So the countdown began. My days would start off with heart eye emoji-filled messages from Conor and *"You sure you really want to do this?"* texts from Luella. As the days crept on, though, my excitement started to infect Luella who had never actually been to Ireland before.

"*I don't even really like Guinness, but we need to go to the factory!"* she randomly exclaimed one day.

"*What's a trip there without Guinness from the OG headquarters?"* I replied.

Then I remembered that I needed to let Kieran and Finn know that I was returning. Kieran's promise was accurate in that "it wasn't the end." And so, I told him that I would be coming back to Ireland, this time with a friend, and staying in Dublin... with Conor.

"What are ye doing?" he questioned.

I started to type out: *"Well, I think me and Conor might be something and..."* but I quickly realized how utterly ridiculous that would probably sound. I couldn't backspace that entire sentence quick enough. Now with a blank textbox, I instead typed back: *"You know, I just wanted to come back, and he offered me his place."*

"You could've at least let me know, and I could've found ye a better place in Killarney," he replied. *"Good for you though, girl! Will you be visiting down here?"*

Great question, Kieran. I actually had no idea what the week-long trip would entail.

Amidst my back-and-forth conversation with Kieran, I realized that I also had to inform my mom that, *well*, her daughter was leaving the country and heading back to Ireland with Luella. She was a little upset that I was going on such short notice, but she trusted Luella. She couldn't quite understand why I was going back there when there were so many other countries that I mentioned wanting to travel to, but I just shrugged it off as wanting to experience St. Patrick's Day in the land of the leprechauns.

And so, before I knew it, the day came when Luella and I were boarding the plane to Dublin. I sent a picture of the flight information to Conor just before take-off so that he could track the flight. In a little over six hours and thirty minutes, we'd be shimmying out of our crammed seats and stepping foot in one of my favorite cobblestone cities. I figured that I would pass the time by sleeping so that when we arrived—which would be around 6:30 a.m. given the time differ-ence—I'd feel well-rested. (That's a joke because no matter how hard I try, I've never felt relaxed after a flight—especially in non-extra-legroom economy seats.) A glorious curveball was thrown my way when the attendant came down the aisle asking if we'd like any wine.

"Wait, for free?" I asked.

Once the attendant laughed and replied that it was, indeed, free, Luella and I both gave each other that *look.* You know, that look when you can somehow communicate with your best friend as if you have that twin telepathy magic. With just a few quick blinks back-and-forth, we both non-verbally agreed to commence our journey with two plastic cups containing cheap sweet red—but we also seemed to agree that we should only have one round and get some rest.

"Cheers!" she joyfully said.

"Sláinte!" I replied back. *"That's how they say cheers out there!"*

Instead of casually sipping our wines, we both gave each other that *look* again and somehow mentally agreed to have an impromptu chugging contest. Though a bit of wine dribbled down both of our chins, I'll give it to Luella on that round. The whiteness of our teeth now softened by hues of red and giggles beginning to brew in our bellies, we rang the "assistance needed" button and got our refills while our attendant chuckled and made a comment that she knew she'd be frequenting our row quite a bit. She was right. For the next few hours, we got absolutely obliterated.

Drunk, tired, and in desperate need of a good teeth brushing, Luella and I slugged our way out of the gate toward the baggage claim. I turned on my phone to a few dozen messages from Conor. The first handful of messages were rather cute in nature saying that he couldn't wait to see us and that he had planned for us to go to a whiskey-tasting event in the afternoon. (Uck, I couldn't bear to drink another drop of liquor.) As the texts went on, though, you could tell that he grew a bit agitated because apparently our flight was delayed, which seemed to "ruin" his morning. In all honesty, this was news to me because I was too wine-whacked to even pay attention to any of the pilot's in-flight announcements. A quick look at my watch did confirm, though, that we were running about fifty minutes late—and we still needed to wait for our suitcases.

Oh well, it's not like I can control the wind patterns and, in all fairness, I did give him the flight number, I thought to myself.

His last message stated that he was tired of waiting, had coffee ready for us (which was now cold and also bothered him), and wanted to just "get the day started already."

He changes his tune quickly and gets annoyed at something seemingly small.

RATIONALIZING THE RED FLAG: *"He was clearly so excited to see me and every minute he had to wait made him more and more disappointed. He's not agitated... he's just so bummed."*

WHAT I SHOULD'VE DONE: Pointed out that this is nothing to get upset about.

I FORGIVE MYSELF FOR: Not saying what I was thinking.

IF IT HAPPENS AGAIN: I will change my plans if he changes his tune.

SELF-LOVE LESSON: Emotional intelligence is important. I will work on mine and deserve a partner who works on his.

"Started?" Luella questioned. *"Noooo way. He can't be serious! It's sooooo early, girl."*

Once we located our bags on the carousel and hoisted them up with the little energy that we had left, we made our way to the "car pick-ups" section and looked for my serendipitous soulmate. And so, when a scrawny man with sloped shoulders, gray-dusted red hair, and a crooked cigarette-stained smile approached me and tried to give me a kiss, I was completely thrown off guard (and simultaneously scared).

"Oh, guess we're just at the hugging stage for now," the man awkwardly joked.

Oh my god, it's Conor! I thought to myself as I haphazardly gave into his hug with distance, concern, and hesitation. He looked nothing like I remembered… and nothing like any of the smiling selfies that he'd shared with me.

He then guided us toward his car. This man was the full-on hare in this race, whereas Luella and I were the tortoises. He was not pleased with our exhaustion and kept trying to encourage us to "stop dragging our feet."

"I thought you said he was cute!" Luella laughed at a whisper-level volume.

"I… could've sworn he was cute!" I said. *"I can't believe he's aged this poorly…"*

"Or… it must've been the beer goggles," she laughed back.

"Definitely the beer goggles," I joked. *"And he's a pro at photo editing."*

As we approached the car, he started to explain how he had the entire day planned with eating, drinking and then soccer-watching at one of the major bars in town. I gave Luella that *look* again, and we both knew that we needed sleep.

"Conor, is it okay if we just take a quick nap? We didn't get much sleep," I shared.

"I took off this entire week for you… and you want to sleep?" he snapped back.

"Whoa!" I said.

"Ye must forgive me," he said. *"I'm just cranky."*

He drove off as a lullaby of the rain hitting the windows ever so gently and the soft smacking of the windshield wipers nearly put Luella

and me to sleep. Maybe I'd wake up and it'd all just be a dream…
except, my imagination couldn't have even fathomed what was to come
next. Now remember, I've been to Ireland before and drove around
the entire country. I remember what Dublin looked like—and he was
slowly creeping out of the city into an unknown area. (Again, I am
directionally challenged, but I do remember prominent food markers
and bars.) Beautiful infrastructure was turning more ragged with each
swivel down a new street. In front of our eyes now laid crumbled
buildings, graffitied walls, littered corners, and broken windows. We
were entering the slums.

"I thought you said you lived in the heart of Dublin," I commented.

"Well, I'm just on the outskirts," he said. *"We're almost there."*

The car slowed as it approached a decrepit, withered house that
had a bed sheet sloppily pinned to the front window as a curtain. As
he watched Luella and me struggle to carry our suitcases out of his
car, he told us that this was our home for the next week and to make
ourselves as comfortable as possible. He then escorted us to the front
door before telling us to *"Shhhh!"*

"I thought you lived alone?" I questioned.

As the door creaked open, a frayed, foul-smelling dog limped past
our feet to go lick some water out of a mud puddle in the front yard.
Not even two seconds later, we heard shouts from an angry old woman
who appeared to be upstairs. She yelled, *"TAKE YOUR SHOES OFF!"*
Without hesitation, Luella and I ripped our shoes off thinking that
this lady reminded us of Miss Trunchbull from *Matilda* based off of
her tone alone.

Conor then motioned for us to enter the room to the right. The
room appeared to be an old dining room that was converted into a
last-minute bedroom based on the chipped wood flooring and awkward
broken fireplace staring at us from the center of the wall. In front of
the fireplace directly on the floor were eight acorns in the shape of a

semi-circle as some form of an odd decoration—or maybe a satanic ritual (I'm still not entirely sure to this day). In the far left corner he had a mattress thrown on the ground null of any type of bed frame. A thin blue blanket was sprawled along its surface as it lazily tried to meet the corners. Then, there were two crumpled and heavily dented pillows thrown into the mattress's middle. In the other corner he had a TV tray with a laptop on it and a lawn chair propped directly in front of that—which I only assumed was his work station. He then had one dresser directly near that set-up with clothes hanging out of the drawers and several used soft drink bottles scattered across its top.

"*Where are Luella and I supposed to sleep?*" I questioned.

He said, "*I didn't get that far, but we have a couch or…*"

"*Absolutely not,*" I interrupted. "*Me and her are sticking together.*"

"*Well, I guess for now, ye can sleep on the mattress, and we'll figure out the rest later,*" he said as he walked over to the dresser, yanked out a towel from one of the piles, and spread it on the floor as if he was about to catch a tan on the beach. He then stole one of the pillows from the bed and propped it near the head of the towel and moved his laptop right in front of that.

"*Ye can nap right now, and I'll just watch a movie,*" he said.

I didn't have enough time to fully comprehend where I was or what was happening—but all I kept thinking to myself was, *Wow, I'm glad Luella is here.* I tried texting a few friends, but Ireland's WiFi at the time was incredibly lousy. It took about twenty minutes to send one single text to Scarlett begging her to please find and book us two plane tickets home.

As Conor left the room to go use the bathroom, Luella looked at me and said, "*Brianna, my girl, what the absolute hell is this?*"

"*I think it's actually hell,*" I panicked.

"*I think I need some sleep before I can even start thinking about this,*" she laughed. That's one thing I have always admired about Luella: she always finds laughter and positivity even in the worst of situations, which always seems to help counteract my anxiety.

Luella jumped on the mattress while simultaneously lifting the blanket—and within seconds she was encased in what appeared to be a mini dust storm.

"Ew, what the f..." Luella managed to say before I *shhhhh!*ed her.

She then looked a bit closer at the pillowcase. There were white flakes scattered all over its surface.

"Brianna, I'm about to vomit!" she said as she dry-heaved.

"Please don't tell me that's…" I gagged.

"It's dandruff, Brianna," she coughed out.

"I'm so skeeved!" I nearly vomited. *"I can't do this!"*

"Brianna, we need to get a quick nap in and then figure this out while we're out and have WiFi at a pub or something," she said as she walked over to his dresser, pulled out another towel, and placed it on top of the blanket and pillowcase.

A few moments later, Conor re-entered the room. He made his way over to his gawky towel, faced belly-down in the opposite direction of us, plugged his headphones in, and then watched whatever he had queued up on his laptop. I made my way over to the towel, snuggled up next to Luella, and prayed to the acorn gods (or demons) that I would somehow get cell service while Luella took a quick nap.

Thankfully, I would get pops of service every once in a while so that I could connect with Scarlett. I briefly told her the situation but asked her to please hold off on asking anymore questions in fear of losing signal. The main priority right now was escaping. When my web pages would load I was able to find some hotels, but the prices were astronomical being that we were visiting during the country's craziest celebratory week. Honestly, I didn't even care about the cost that I would incur for either a flight back or a hotel for the next few days—I just wanted to leave (and shower). Each time that I would get close to securing a room, though, the internet would completely black out again.

Simultaneously, I tried to text Kieran, but he probably was still sleeping since it was still pretty early in the morning. *"I NEED YOUR HELP PLEASE!"* I texted. I didn't even realize that he'd probably wake up in panic from these texts. (Kieran, I'm so sorry.)

I fought with my phone for nearly one hour until Luella rolled over and whispered that she needed to get out of this "skeevatzy" room. (We now forever refer to each other as "Skeevatz," which is an Italian-American slang term—maybe used by just us—to describe something that's disgusting.) I couldn't have agreed more. I made my way over to Conor, tapped him on the shoulder, and asked him if we could get the day started. Though it was still relatively early in the morning, there's always one thing to do in Ireland regardless of the time: drink. Luella and I made our way over to the tiny half-bathroom hidden under the rickety wooden staircase with missing treads. We barely squeezed in together—it was almost as if we were playing a game of Chubby Bunny and we were the marshmallows, and the bathroom was the mouth. We sat there, like pure filth, and brushed our teeth as we looked at our reflections through the grime-caked mirror.

"So much for him being a neat freak," Luella managed to laugh.

Though all we craved was a shower, Luella and I both agreed that we'd rather go bathe in that mud puddle outside than in whatever contraption Conor probably had. Instead, we quickly asked Conor if we could use the room to change into something that didn't have a lingering airplane stench to it—or potentially have traces of dandruff. We placed those clothes in one of the garbage bags that I packed for dirty laundry, misted ourselves with some body spray, applied deodorant, and threw on some hats.

"This is the grossest I've ever felt," I whispered. *"I feel like I need to douse myself in bleach."*

He exaggerates his living situation and/or tells white lies to cover up his current circumstances.

RATIONALIZING THE RED FLAG: *"He just wanted to seem cool—you know, like he lived in Dublin in his own place. He was probably embarrassed, and, after all, he wanted to impress me."*

WHAT I SHOULD'VE DONE: Asked for a working phone and called a cab to get the hell out of here, because this definitely ain't Dublin. (Also I probably shouldn't have gone to another country to stay with a man I had only met once...)

I FORGIVE MYSELF FOR: Settling for less than I deserve.

IF IT HAPPENS AGAIN: I will leave. Full stop.

SELF-LOVE LESSON: Truth is important. Stretching the truth and telling little lies leads to big disasters. It is an act of self-love to demand honesty.

Our day of drinking began at around 10 a.m. Conor took us over to the Irish Whiskey Museum and, though liquor was the last thing that either of us wanted, Luella and I decided to indulge. The bartenders loved our American accents and continued to fill our glasses with Powers Gold Label, Jameson, and Tullamore Dew. The more drunk we grew, the less gross we felt. It was a nice shift in the dynamic. Conor mingled with a few locals while Luella and I laughed and tried to seduce the bartender for their protected WiFi password. Though it was for employee purposes only, we did manage to get the WhiskeyLover123! password for a measly single bar of service. The second my phone connected to this power source, it lit up like a Christmas tree with notifications.

"A one-way ticket home is $1,100 a person," Scarlett texted. *"Do you really want to book that?"*

"Girl, are ye okay?" Kieran texted.

"Hey, are you there safe, Bri?" my mom questioned.

"I found a 1-star bed and breakfast for $70 a night in Dublin," Scarlett sent.

I immediately connected with Kieran and told him of our situation. He said that he couldn't really help out in Dublin, but if we hopped on a train to Killarney he could work out some accommodations. I told him that we were out right now trying to connect to WiFi and didn't have our bags, but that if we were to stay in Ireland and not fly home, I would take him up on that offer. I then texted Scarlett back asking her to book a one night stay at that bed and breakfast and promised that I would give her the money I owed her the second that I got home. I felt relieved… until I realized the text kept failing to send. I tried to connect to the internet myself, but it took nearly ten minutes to load one single page.

Once our whiskey-tasting ended, Conor took us over to a local WiFi-less pub for some more drinks. As frustrated as I was at the situation, you can only be so down when you're surrounded by a sea of people dancing, laughing, and clanking their pint glasses together. We stayed with Conor for a bit and then decided to go venture out on our own and explore the bar. Similar to the whiskey bar, dozens of locals kept buying Luella and me drinks to welcome us into their country during "the merriest week ever." Once the drinks started pouring at a much steadier speed, Luella and I found ourselves blitzed once more. The two of us befriended this gentleman named Liam. We explained our situation to him and he called us "silly Americans" as he laughed as he ordered us more rounds of Smithwick's Pale Ale.

At one point, we didn't even realize that most of the people sitting at the bar made their way outside to watch the Ireland versus England Six Nations rugby tournament being projected against one of the pub's massive side walls. (Ireland ended up destroying England's Grand Slam dream—adding even more excitement to the week.) Liam told us that we should follow him outside to partake in the *craic*. When we stepped outside we noticed that the sun was basically gone. We allowed the day to escape us when what we really needed to do was escape the day.

"Nice of ye to show up," Conor sarcastically joked.

Liam pulled me to the side and questioned, *"Wait, that's who ye with? He's some thick bollocks."*

I assume that my face signaled confusion so he quickly clarified, *"That guy's a tool."*

Out of the corner of my eye I saw that Luella started yawning. She gave me that *look* again. I understood her exactly: we were jetlagged, dirty, and in need of a clean place to crash. I approached Conor and asked him if we could maybe head back to his place for some rest. His face turned redder than some of the hair colors that bobbed around me.

"This is an absolute joke!" he screamed. *"I took off of work for ye, and I'm not going back. This is SHITE!"*

"WHOA!" Luella snarled back. *"Who do you think you're talking to?"*

I disappointedly looked over at Liam who then immediately interjected. He angrily pulled Conor to the side and yelled at him in some of the fastest spoken words I have ever heard (but couldn't quite understand). I then saw Conor reach into his pockets, hand us over the keys to his room, and write down his address on a bar napkin. Conor stormed to the back of the crowd and left my depth of vision.

"I told ya," Liam said. *"A tool."*

Liam brought us back inside over to the bartender who called us a taxi. He then proceeded to give us his contact information and told us that if we ended up staying in Dublin, we could go out for some more healthy *craic*. Just as I was hugging Liam goodbye, I felt my phone buzz. Apparently, my text to Scarlett was finally sent. She booked us that 1-star room with WiFi, and we could check-in tomorrow at 11 a.m. We just had to survive one more night.

Just as the taxi was dropping us off at his dilapidated house, I asked if I could reserve a ride in the morning to our new stay. He said that he would arrive promptly at 10:30 a.m. and then shook on it to keep his promise. He also gave me his personal WhatsApp number just in case. Luella and I tiptoed through the house so that we wouldn't disturb the beast upstairs, found another towel in his dresser, and wrapped ourselves up. We also locked Conor's bedroom door for safety purposes. A few hours later, I did hear tiny knocks on the door as he tried to get us to let him in—but I guess he understood that he would be sleeping on the couch. We didn't open the door again until 10:20 a.m. when we went to squish back into the bathroom for a quick teeth brushing.

Conor embarrassingly made his way over into his room. *"I'm so sorry,"* he said. *"I had a bit too much to drink, you see."*

He uses alcohol as a crutch for his outlandish, aggressive behavior.

RATIONALIZING THE RED FLAG: Yeah, there's no more rationalizing this shit...

WHAT I SHOULD'VE DONE: Exactly what I'm about to do.

I FORGIVE MYSELF FOR: Nothing. I handled this situation like I should've in the first place.

IF IT HAPPENS AGAIN: I will do exactly the same thing.

SELF-LOVE LESSON: It is a sign of self-love to leave a risky situation. Plus, alcohol is no excuse for bad behavior. (This clearly is a common theme.)

Luella and I both ignored him. He must've noticed that we looked unphased and determined to leave based on the positioning of our bags near the front door.

"Where are ye going?" he then questioned. *"Ye don't have to leave. I'm sorry."*

"Conor, your behavior has been utterly disgusting," I said. *"You lied about everything. Who you are, where you live, what you do... we're leaving!"*

Before he could even attempt to refute my statement, the gray minivan with the yellow stripe reading "Taxi" pulled up like a beacon of sunshine on this dreary drizzle-filled day. *Just in time,* I thought.

We entered the taxi and I immediately blocked Conor from every possible source of connection—wiping my existence from his social channels. Luella and I chatted about what we were going to do. A part of us wanted to go home, but a part of us wanted to stay. A short while into our drive, the taxi driver pulled over to the side of the road, pointed out to the River Liffey (which flows through the center of Dublin), and said, *"Look!"* During our conversation, Luella and I didn't even notice that the clouds seemed to break and the sun was pumping sunshine ever so graciously into the heart of Dublin—and gifted us with a beautiful double rainbow that spanned across the horizon.

"Now that's lucky, girls!" the driver said. *"Ye don't get that often."*

We stepped outside of the taxi, inhaled in the fresh air, exhaled any potential leftover dandruff that may have slipped into our nostrils, and gave each other that *look*. It was a sign. We were going to stay and figure this out.

"That's a better looking semi-circle than the acorns!" I giggled. Luella bellied over in laughter.

"And who the fuck was that older woman yelling at us?" I laughed.

"That is yet another mystery," Luella laughed.

And so, like the nomads that we were, we hotel-hopped for the rest of our days in Ireland—making our way from Dublin to Belfast and even back to Killarney (to reunite with Kieran and Finn) by train. Despite feeling so lost, I felt so at peace.

It was one of the most spontaneous and liberating experiences of my life. To thank Luella for not letting me do this alone, I charged mostly all of the stays to my card. I didn't calculate spending hundreds of dollars on accommodations, but I knew that I could pay it off if I just laid low for the two weeks following our arrival back in the States and used my paychecks for these purposes alone. For one of the first times in my life, I had to let go of this feeling of having to "control" everything. It was frightening, but I let Luella's free spirit grab my soul's hand and dance in the winds that carried us.

Looking Within at Personal
RED FLAGS

- You turn to unhealthy behaviors (such as drinking or running away) to escape your true feelings.

- You tend to over-romanticize people, places, and things.

- You allow a rom-com to manipulate your feelings about a person or situation.

- You disclose your personal information to a not-so-personal (or trusted) individual.

- You hop on a plane to the other side of the world for a guy you barely know.

- Your mental health went undiagnosed and unhealed for several years.

- You make plans to stay at a stranger's house without any backup plan.

find that I wasn't just obsessed with the validation from food, but the validation from earning nothing but A's, too. My mom wasn't one of those parents who would be upset if I brought home bad grades, either, as long as I truly gave it my all. Instead, it was more of a self-induced fulfillment. Knowing that I was achieving A's gave me this drive. It made me feel secure in myself.

The same couldn't be said for my brother. Though my brother was (and still is) the kindest and purest of souls, my brother couldn't seem to comprehend ideas or communicate. His first spoken words were *"duck, duck, goose"* and that was at such a delayed age that it concerned his pediatrician. He was extremely picky with food and textures, too, and it resulted in a diet that consisted of pizza, pasta, breaded chicken tenders, and French fries. He was also incredibly shy and socially awkward. After some developmental testing, it was revealed that my brother was on the lower end of the autism spectrum. As it was explained to my mom, my brother's mind and mental state wouldn't age in congruence with his physical body. In other words, my brother could be thirty with the mental maturity of a thirteen-year-old.

My stepdad couldn't seem to understand nor accept not having a "normal" son. As his rage continued, so did my coping with overindulgence. I also started to follow his lead and grow angry at my situation, too. I couldn't understand why I didn't have a "normal" brother at the time and why he couldn't play with me like other kids. I would grow so irate that I couldn't have a friend or someone to turn to in the chaos that was my home aside from my Barbie or *NSYNC marionette dolls that I began to distance myself within the walls of my room. I even looked forward to the days that I had school so that I could be surrounded by kids my age.

This has become a theme that has strung throughout my childhood into my early adulthood: I lived isolated in a room to myself in a house that was filled with roommates—and the dynamic worsened with age. The four of us (or sometimes five or six depending on if we had any welcomed guests in our home from our extended family or friend circle who needed help "getting back on their feet") would cross paths sometimes in the kitchen, but that was it. We didn't have "family" dinners. We didn't really have a "family." Even after my stepdad fully committed himself to therapy to completely work on healing his own heart-shattering traumas, curb his anger (which he did after some time), and dedicate himself to being a better, kinder man to our family, I never really formed that relationship with him... or my brother... or my real father.

Interestingly enough, I remember watching *The Fresh Prince of Bel-Air* as a child and, though I didn't understand much of the humor, two things did resonate with me at the time:

- I found Will Smith to be a hunk and I developed a massive childhood crush on him. In fact, I would beg my mom to mail him handwritten letters professing my love along with wallet-sized school-year pictures.

- When I stumbled across that iconic episode, *Papa's Got a Brand New Excuse,* where Will looks at Uncle Phil and asks, *"How come he don't want me, man?"* as his dad let him down (again), I felt those emotions and cried to myself at such a young age. I couldn't comprehend it at the time, but Will was able to articulate the exact inner emotions that I felt on so many levels.

My dad eventually moved on to get remarried... twice. His second wife, Lisa (which is also my mother's name) was a really sweet and kind woman. When my father would actually pick me up and drive me to their home in Pennsylvania, she would be the one occupying me for the majority of that time. It wasn't too long into their marriage that she found out that she was pregnant. My father used this news to further propel me into neglect. Once my half-brother Bryce was born, I became obsolete. (Hey, at least he finally got the boy that he always wanted. My Pop took this secret to his grave, but it recently came to light that when I was born, my father briskly walked outside of the hospital, lit a cigarette, and disappointedly muttered, *"Dammit, a girl"* under his breath right in front of my grandfather.) It did break my heart seeing him be a father when that's all I ever wanted from him—but I guess you could say that karma bit him when, after nearly three years of being in Bryce's life, he found out that he was not, in fact, the father. (To all of my readers, I hope you read that in your best Maury voice.) Once this happened, my father completely disappeared from my life and he couldn't be found—with the exception of one final instance when I was sixteen.

I was cheerleading in the bleachers at a high school basketball game and sitting next to Lizzy when this random scrawny, older-looking gentleman with a sunken, ashy face approached me.

"Hey," the man muttered.

"Excuse me, sir, you can't be sitting here," I replied. *"This is for the cheerleaders only."* Lizzy looked over at me with curious eyes.

"Brianna, you don't know who I am?" the man questioned.

"Am I supposed to?" I awkwardly responded.

"It's me... your dad," he replied.

I genuinely did not recognize him—which was both disappointing and heartbreaking. I immediately locked eyes with my coach who sensed the panic consuming me like the symbiote that took over Venom. Without explanation and null of a response to my father, I darted from the bleachers and ran straight into the locker room. I didn't realize that Lizzy had followed me until I felt a hand pull me back from completely bolting out of the high school. She grabbed me and gave me the warmest of hugs. The two of us left that game early and exchanged rather poignant words about our absent fathers.

I never saw or heard from my father again—unless, of course, you consider a legal notice from his lawyer sent to my house two years later as communication stating that he had emancipated me so as to not have to help pay for my college tuition. He's now gone on to marry a third wife—and, according to his online profile, he's a loving stepfather and step-granddad. (Curse you, Facebook, for showing his profile under my "Suggested Friends" list.)

For some reason, I still can't wrap my head around how someone could have a child (and a pretty good one at that) and let that half of yourself grow up parentless. It's always been this void in my heart that I've tried to fill. The one thing that I find comfort in, though, is that a lot of you reading this probably have some form of a daddy issue, too. It doesn't make it right—but this dark camaraderie of sorts keeps me from spiraling.

Later in my adult years, I even began trying to heal this abandonment issue by calling any and every man "daddy" who seemed like a strong, masculine, powerful individual—but not in Sigmund Freud's Oedipus complex-like way. Instead, it was a message to myself of security that I have found a potential protector. Not trying to spoil the ending or anything, but that clearly backfired as I charged after red flags faster than a bull toward a matador.

THE RED *Room*

- What key lessons did you take away from Part II?

- Did you fall for any of the red flags that I fell for in Part II? If so, which ones?

- Did you notice any red flags that I didn't point out in Part II? If so, what were they? What might you have done in that situation?

- Have you ever been cheated on in the past? If so, how did that make you feel?

- Have you ever cheated on a partner? If so, what were the motivating factors behind those actions?

- Has someone ever manipulated conversations to make you feel at fault for their negative behaviors? Reflect on how that felt.

- Have you ever mistakenly thought you were in love? If so, when did you realize you weren't experiencing actual love?

- Speaking of love, how do you define that word? What does a healthy, loving relationship actually look like to you?

- Have you ever let the "love" word make you stay in a relationship for much longer than you probably should have?

- What's the "craziest" thing you've ever done for love?

- Do you or have you ever allowed substances to cloud your judgment as it pertained to pursuing a potential person? If so, how did that turn out in the end?

- What's your relationship with your parents like? Would you consider it healthy or unhealthy—and why?

- Do you have positive relationship role models that you can look up to? If not, do you think that has impacted your choices in partners in the past?

Part Three

ROCK BOTTOM

[ˈräk ˈbädəm]

ADJECTIVE

1. at the lowest possible level

2. well below normal

MOMENTS

[ˈmōmənts]

PLURAL NOUN

1. a very brief period of time

2. of importance

9

THE GUY WITH THE GIRLFRIEND

If you were to tell me that it was possible to look into someone's soul by simply peering into said person's eyes (and nothing else), I might respond with some skepticism. And if you were to further state that you could tell, by some reason unbeknownst to you, that you had this undeniable magnetic connection without having really talked to said person, I would ask which strain you were smoking this week.

Yes, I'm a romanticist. The "love at first sight" thing, though, I never could quite wrap my head around. Don't get me wrong, every time I'm out with my friends and I notice a handsome guy walk by, I'll joke that it was my soulmate number *insert triple-digit number here* and I am in love. Obviously, that's a joke (sort of). But let me tell you, that whole thinking-you-could-love-someone-with-just-a-look thing may very well be true.

It was during my first year working in the communications department at a hospital that I met **him**. My first project was to assist in the creation of a series of live virtual webinars focused on "prepping for your next procedure" and "post-surgical care" for patients currently hoping to treat their orthopedic pain. Essentially, I had to logistically set up and direct some of these demonstrations and help manage any questions being thrown out in the chat sections by the public. I collaborated with clinical experts scattered throughout the facility in addition to a team of event planners and IT folks, with the main lead from the tech department being a guy named Nick.

Two days before our first live session, Nick had to abruptly cancel as another priority IT project apparently crept onto his calendar. I relayed the information over to the care team. Let's just say, the team wasn't happy being told that they'd cleared an entire day of patient appointments for a now-defunct plan. We also had upwards of one hundred individuals registered to attend the event. I escalated this to my leaders as I actively sought their insight.

A few hours later, I found out that a close relative had unexpectedly passed away. I took the rest of the day off—and the following day for bereavement.

They'll just have to figure this out, I thought to myself.

I received frantic calls, emails, and text messages from my leaders while in bereavement trying to promptly recover from this blunder. I had to work while I had taken off for mourning. So there I was, grieving a loss in the family and hopping on back-and-forth conference calls. We recruited another team from the IT department of a different hospital within our network to pull the weight that was dropped by Nick. Beautiful

Flustered, I went in for the first webinar recording and was so distraught by what my leaders had put me through that I didn't care. I really didn't contribute to the job. I simply was a body in the room as I watched the team do their thing.

"Sure, the lighting looks great," I'd negligently assure one of my colleagues.

I was in and out. The next day, I had to go back and record a second webinar. This time, I had to meet and work with Nick for the first time. It was because of him that I harbored all of this resentment, or so I thought.

Again, I didn't care. I slicked my hair back into a tight bun, threw on a schluppy navy blue dress, strapped on some heels, and headed over to the hospital. As I was on my way, I opened my phone to text Nick that I would be arriving in about ten minutes. As I was about to press "send," my phone rang. It was Nick.

"Hey, I'll be over there in about ten minutes!" he exclaimed.

"No way! I was just about to text you the same thing!" I laughed. We were both arriving way earlier than needed. Weird.

For this particular webinar, we scheduled the streaming to take place in an operating room while we featured one of the unit's most prominent surgeons. I officially met Nick as we both exited the opposite-facing locker rooms near the operating room while wearing our sterilized "bunny suits" and face masks that hid all of our features (with the only exception, of course, being our eyes). Though completely in disguise, there was something about his overall demeanor that signaled to me that he was incredibly handsome.

This is unprofessional, Brianna, snap out of it, I thought to myself. *Besides, you're supposed to hate him—he canceled on you last minute.*

We slowly stopped walking as we approached the double doors to the operating room. As we turned toward one another and locked eyes, I felt like the entire world stopped and we were the main characters in some kind of movie. Imagine this: the foreground went completely out of focus and the only subject I could see in its greatest detail was Nick. My heart was screaming—it felt as if it had just gotten a glimpse of finding its home without even understanding how this experience was possible.

Ashton Kutcher, I thought Punk'd was canceled, so you can go home now, I joked to myself as I tried to downplay the feeling.

Besides, his entire face was masked. This couldn't be real. Maybe it was just my sex-fiending kitty that sniffed out his testosterone.

He then broke my trance once he started talking to me, ever so effortlessly, as we entered the room and started arranging the equipment. There was an absolute instant connection in terms of conversation. Typically, I'd get nervous when talking to someone I found attractive. However, in this case I felt completely natural. Weird again. Nick then whipped out his phone and said that we had to take a selfie to document the moment. The picture of us in our purple hair bonnets, black and white bunny suits, and white masks while throwing up our respective peace signs is one I will never delete from my camera roll.

We met the doctor, event team, and other clinical leads after several minutes. I watched as he seemed to crochet together the wiring for all of the equipment and check the pulse of the connection that he had just created. (You'd think I was watching some kind of hot, nerdy IT-like Dr. Frankenstein as he yelled, *"It's alive!"* when the internet didn't lag.) We laughed, high-fived, and made quite the powerful team. The doctor even remarked what great partners we were.

Once we wrapped up the webinar, we made our ways to the locker rooms and changed. Again, we both exited the locker rooms at the same time and met in the middle of the hallway. I finally saw his wildly handsome and smooth face—and I couldn't help but smile. (Hopefully I didn't blush.) He was absolute magic—but I also didn't want to get my hopes up if this man wasn't feeling anything. Plus, we're coworkers.

We both exited the hospital and sat down at a bench near the front of the building. As the light shimmered off of his Dominican skin, we exchanged interests and quickly found ourselves divulging stories of world travel

"I've run with bulls throughout the streets of Spain," he said.

"I swam with elephants in a river in Thailand," I responded.

He was so cultured. Even hotter.

"So, do you want to grab a bite to eat?" Nick asked.

He's your coworker.

RATIONALIZING THE RED FLAG: *"It's worked out for some people... no?"*

WHAT I SHOULD'VE DONE: Kept it professional.

I FORGIVE MYSELF FOR: Not setting stronger boundaries.

IF IT HAPPENS AGAIN: I will focus on the work at-hand and keep the banter to a minimum. You'll see how I don't exactly do that...

SELF-LOVE LESSON: I need not look for love—especially in the wrong places. Instead, I can relax and let love naturally gravitate towards me.

Of course I wanted to. *"But is this, like, a coworker thing or…"* I snapped myself out of spiraling into a realm of overthinking. (Thankfully I didn't say that out loud.) He didn't live in the area, so I suggested a local sushi spot. Plus, they have a killer happy hour menu.

I arrived a few minutes earlier than he did so I grabbed an outdoor table. Once he met me and sat down, we started talking ever so frankly about life again. I told him about the time I flew to Ireland thinking that I met my soulmate. He told me about the time that he was in Cuba with his ex-girlfriend and saw she was still texting her ex, so they broke up. (*"You just can't be friends with an ex,"* he said.) I then mentioned the times I tried to skydive on three separate occasions that were canceled for three different reasons (I heeded that as a warning to never attempt skydiving—it just didn't seem like it was meant to be). He then showed me all of his tattoos. I then told him that I had always wanted to cage dive with a great white shark. We laughed. We even cried. (No, literally. I made Nick try some super spicy edamame, and I guess his palette couldn't hack it. He started crying and simultaneously choking. I think I started crying from laughing so hard.) He even made a remark that our first "real" date could be us "skydiving into shark-infested waters and landing in a cage in water off the coast of Ireland."

Uhm, he just said the 'date' word, I thought. *He must be feeling the same things I'm feeling.*

I walked into my car after our hangout only to immediately dial Kayleigh and say, *"Biiiiiiitch, I think I met my soulmate."*

"Which number are we on now?" she giggled.

"No, you don't get it. I feel something I've never felt before," I said as I recalled every single detail.

From that point on, we texted nonstop. It felt so normal to have him be a part of my daily routine. Given past experiences, though, I didn't want to get my hopes up. That was, until he started sending me shirtless pictures of himself post-workouts. (I'd swoon.) I'd send him selfies back. Once the heart eye and water drop emojis started entering the text thread, I knew that this was more than just a friendly conversation.

About one week later Nick tried requesting me on Instagram. I didn't want to seem overly excited, so I let the notification sit for a few days. When I finally accepted him and went to request him back myself, he suddenly texted me a warning: *"I don't want to scare you, but I have a girlfriend."*

"What?!" I questioned.

"I'm not a cheater," he stated. *"But I'd be lying if I said that I wasn't confused by my feelings for you."*

"Like a moth to a flame I'm drawn to you," he later added. He was saying exactly what I felt.

We'd go back-and-forth as we discussed our crazy attraction to one another. We missed each other after a few days and decided to meet up at a local Mexican restaurant. There I found out that he had secret dancing skills and apparently loves to drunkenly sing karaoke. Then we texted for a few days. After both expressing how much we'd miss each other again, we'd decide to walk a trail near his house together. There, we found out we both were educators outside of work—I taught at a college and he helped software students learn how to code (and it's alluring to find someone on your level). We'd text again. Then we'd meet up and hike a different trail as we openly talked about this insane sexual chemistry between us and detailed how we'd "do it" in the park. (We even had two loving deer—one doe and one buck—happily prance in front of us, stop in the middle of the trail merely a few feet away, and look at us. Seriously, directly in our eyes. We both felt the sign. *Those fackin' deer,*" he remarked.) Then we'd text. And again. And again.

"I really want you to myself," I finally admitted.

He's in a relationship.

RATIONALIZING THE RED FLAG: *"It's complicated... and we can't fight the chemistry!"*

WHAT I SHOULD'VE DONE: Stopped it immediately.

I FORGIVE MYSELF FOR: Wanting the comfort of a man regardless if he had a girlfriend or not.

IF IT HAPPENS AGAIN: I will not allow myself to be "the other woman." Fuck that.

SELF-LOVE LESSON: If I want my relationships to be seen as sacred, I must view other people's relationships as sacred. It's all a mirror. Allowing a man with a girlfriend to continue flirting with me is not fair to me or to the other woman. I love myself more than to be a mistress.

He invited me over to his apartment where he lived with a few other roommates who just so happened to be out of town.

"I'm not like this," he said. *"But I can't pretend this isn't real."*

I was getting ready to leave my house when I received the text message: *"I'm sorry, I can't do this."*

I didn't blame him. I couldn't do it either. I've been cheated on in the past. I couldn't bear to have that guilt weigh on my already broken heart. I told him that we should probably distance ourselves from one another. That lasted about two days when he broke the silence by texting me a picture of his techy classroom followed by: *"Thinking about you."* And so I caved.

It was about a week or two before the start of my semester when I was texting him about the need to start working on my new lesson plan. He reinvited me back to his apartment—but to, you know, "share ideas as one scholar to another." I questioned the validity of this proposition, but when he texted me his address I found myself in my car within minutes.

I was a little awkward at first. I didn't know what to expect. I didn't want to cross any lines, and I didn't want to make any moves (but I also did). I was ready to just let the universe do what it needed to do. He met me outside while wearing his glasses. (*Uuuunf, I want to taste him,* I thought.) He had *Mr. Deeds* (another Sandler classic) queued up on his television screen ready to go. I remember him pressing play and for the next one hour and thirty-six minutes we got lost in each other's words while that provided background noise. We talked and laughed the entire time. Once the movie ended, he put on some music videos from the 1980s. We were dancing to Eddie Murphy's "Party All the Time" at one point. Never in my life have I had so much fun just hanging out with someone on a couch.

At one point, he got up from where he was sitting on the far end of the couch, turned off the light, and made his way toward my side of the couch. He asked me to scooch in so that we could cuddle. We

Looking Within at Personal
RED FLAGS

- You mistake sex (and even lust) for love.

- You look for love anywhere and everywhere.

- You don't respect the boundaries of another relationship enough to stay away.

- You believe that he will leave his partner for you.

- You're acting in a way that you would never want to experience yourself (i.e. being someone else's "secret lover" yet never wanting to be cheated on in a relationship yourself.)

- You try to pretend like pictures of "happy couples" online (especially of a "taken" person that you're into) don't bother you.

⚠ CONTENT WARNING

This next chapter contains stories of sexual abuse as well as narcissistic abuse on mental, emotional, and spiritual levels.

10

THE STONE-COLD NARCISSIST

If Taylor Swift has taught me one valuable life lesson, it's that you can transform any heartbreak into some kind of boppy banger. I call this particular song "Love at First Swipe"—except, well, since my voice sounds more like a drowning hyena whenever I try to hit any note, I decided to save everyone's eardrums and write my own piece of art within the confines of this book binding.

You see, one night Scarlett and I decided to drink some wine and download dating apps. We watched a comedy sketch on these two friends hilariously swapping accounts and swiping on behalf of the other while messaging some potentials. So, we followed suit. I started matching left and right for Scarlett, and she did the same for me.

At one point, she paused and said, *"Whoa, Bri, look! He looks like a lil' artsy papi!"*

There he was in his artistically unique glory. He looked like a mix of several ethnicities (which I later came to find out was mostly Egyptian and Greek) with a mustache and light stubble that grazed his cheekbones and chin. As for his hair, he donned a shoulder-length straight bob that evoked Johnny Depp's famous mane. This was hugged by a wide-brimmed hat and complemented by turtlenecks, blazer jackets, and thigh-hugging jeans. I swear my face turned red taking a peek at this blue-eyed beau, although that could've been from the wine. (I know, I know… it's hard to keep up with my taste. I go from lumberjacks as a whole to Michael Myers to Adam Sandler. Leave me alone, alright? Beauty is in the eye of the ~~fucked up~~ *all-appreciative* beholder.)

After about an hour of left-right thumb exercises, we both passed out cuddling our cheap bottles of Merlot. I woke up the next morning to a few notifications—one of which was from the artsy papi himself, Hunter. He said some kind of movie quote from *The Waterboy* (as my profile mentioned my odd obsession with Sandler films), and I was instantly swooning. I think that I still may have that screenshotted somewhere in my photo library.

We talked. Nonstop. For days. I quite quickly learned that he was a thirty-six-year-old alcoholic in recovery with a little less than one year of sobriety who worked full-time as a barber and part-time as a fashion designer at this up-and-coming clothing store. His forever home was located in the heart of Philadelphia where he grew up with his adoptive Irish Roman Catholic parents and two younger twin sisters.

"I may have felt lost as a kid in not knowing my real identity, but if there's one thing I know for sure, it's that a good cheesesteak is part of my DNA," Hunter laughed.

In addition to raving about his affinity for iconic Philly foods, Hunter wasn't shy in disclosing that he was a semi-religious and political man who was tattooed on every inch of his body from his neck down to his toes, avidly smoked cigarettes, frequently attended jazz shows, and casually played the drums in a punk band.

When he finally asked to take me out on a dinner date I was

drunk at a house party, betting incorrectly on some kind of sporting event, losing tens of thousands of dollars, getting into a verbal fight with Diana, driving home while under the influence, and being called "the devil" by Diana that was the point of no return. He woke up the next morning to see his old silver Impala clumsily parked on his front lawn and the front windshield bashed in—ultimately leading him to surrender to a higher power later that day at an AA meeting.

He's still friends with his ex who he speaks poorly of and wasn't exactly the "best" partner to (and she's still entwined in the family without there being any shared assets or a child).

RATIONALIZING THE RED FLAG: *"He's changed. That was the old him. He would never do that to me because we have a much deeper connection."*

WHAT I SHOULD'VE DONE: Asked him to stop talking in such a poor manner as it pertained to her and left our fling immediately. He clearly had no respect for women or himself.

I FORGIVE MYSELF FOR: Staying.

IF IT HAPPENS AGAIN: I will let him know that nothing he is describing is okay with me and I will end the relationship.

SELF-LOVE LESSON: The way that someone treats others or speaks about others says quite a bit about their character. I didn't initially see that out of my desperation to feel loved. Instead, I need to love myself enough to walk away from any person or situation that doesn't align with the positive, uplifting, high-vibing woman that I strive to be. Oh, and being friends with an ex is okay if there's mutual respect between them, boundaries in place, and honesty with me about the situation. (It's definitely circumstantial, though.)

But that was all in the past, right, and only when he was in active addiction? Well, in a sense, yes. His addiction peeked out in other facets of his life. He was an obsessive gym-goer and would mentally torture himself if he skipped a day—but then in another swing he would binge eat nothing but fried chicken and honey barbecue chips. That, and he was wildly impulsive with no real guidance on saving money (he didn't even have a savings account) or handling it (especially gambling). More than anything, though, he very much clung to the past—in fact, his decrepit Impala that only started with the proper angling of a screwdriver, with a family of birds living in the bush sticking out of his exhaust, was still parked in front of his house.

"It's all part of the master plan," he'd smile as he gently nudged his broken-down car. *"I like to look at these as scattered puzzle pieces toward the grander picture."*

"I get it," I'd smile back at him.

"Plus, I know my grander picture includes you," he'd blush.

When we were together during these first few months, Hunter would tell me how much he adored me and that I was the perfect woman for him. Aside from the sweet talk, what really hooked me was knowing that he had a beautiful heart—but his heart was masked by so many wounded layers of soul-sucking darkness.

To explain, not too long after the holidays, my Pop was diagnosed with cancer. His entire body was being violently attacked. First it was his brain, then his blood, followed by his bones, and, well, the doctors stopped testing after that. I prayed that my stoic hero wouldn't be minimized to a date range in the obituaries. Noticing his rapid deterioration, though, I knew it was only a matter of weeks. January 27th marked the most traumatic day of my life when I received the phone call from my broken mom who muttered the words, *"Bri, I'm so sorry..."* I don't even know what else she said because I mentally checked out and suppressed those memories.

I shut down. I cried every ounce of my body's water weight out. My Pop was a man who was known for putzing around on some kind of do-it-yourself construction project, cooking the meanest of Thanksgiving Day stuffings, and selflessly devoting himself to his family. I wish I could do my Pop better justice in this description, but no master of this craft could properly string together the perfect sentences to showcase his purity.

I remember reaching out to Hunter who told me that I could come over for support. I'm not sure how I made it to his house with my erratic breathing and impaired vision through constant tears, but I somehow found myself walking into his house as his mom and dad engulfed me in warm hugs. Hunter followed this up by instructing me to meet him on the couch and lay on his lap. He leaned over, kissed me on the cheek, offered his condolences, and then soullessly stared at the nightly news. I also still made it a point to congratulate him on another month of sobriety—which became part of my celebratory routine with cards and gifts on each passing 27th.

Two days later, Hunter told me that he couldn't show up to my Pop's wake because he had to "shape-up" some higher-end clients at the shop. When my family and friends went out later that night for small bites to eat post-services and I extended the invitation to Hunter, he told me that he "had a stressful day at work" and "wanted to unwind by himself." He didn't even send a bereavement card to the house for my mom or directly reach out to her—despite him having met her on several occasions prior.

Valentine's Day wasn't too far away. I wasn't in the lovey mood given the hellish events that unfolded, but I still managed to put together the most thoughtful gift basket full of snacks, workout shirts, and hats. Each item had a punny and quirky love note stuffed in a tiny envelope taped to its surface within this basket. So on

Valentine's Day when he, again, had to work, I surprised him with this basket at work (I asked him to meet me in the parking lot). He said he "felt like a jerk" that he didn't get me anything. Not even a bar of chocolate.

He's not there to comfort you on your worst days.

RATIONALIZING THE RED FLAG: I didn't. I didn't rationalize it... I just pushed it under the rug.

WHAT I SHOULD'VE DONE: Realized that real love requires real support when you need it most. I should have ended it there.

I FORGIVE MYSELF FOR: Allowing a less-than-supportive man to play such a significant role in my life.

IF IT HAPPENS AGAIN: I won't tolerate it. I will verbalize my disappointment in a calm and clear way, and then let him know that I deserve better.

SELF-LOVE LESSON: Don't be afraid to let go of toxic individuals. I can be a compassionate and caring human without allowing toxicity into my life.

To make up for it, he scheduled us a date to go to the museum the following week. The entire time we were at the museum, he was Snapchatting pictures and videos of himself in front of artifacts and paintings (null of me) and sending them to his friends—including Mara, who incessantly texted him the entire time. It instantly killed my mood, and I wanted nothing to do with him. Later that night he texted me that he had planned to "officially" ask me to be his girlfriend on our date, but I "ruined it" because of my reaction to something "silly." (This is the beginning of the "devaluation" phase of dating a narcissist, or when your own confidence, self-esteem, and sense of self become void as he takes more control over your power.) I told him that I wanted to go our separate ways. He followed that up by saying, *"But I love you!"* Everything that happened prior to that moment was now scratched from the record. He said that he loved me! So soon! He saw a future with me! So, I stayed...

Except, well, he then held my "silly reaction" against me for months and refused to make the relationship exclusive. In the weeks leading up to Hunter making our relationship "exclusive," he stopped having sex with me as often. At first, we'd hook-up almost every time that we hung out. I realized, though, that his use of foreplay on our second date was to just hook me in as he's only gone down on me about seven more times in our relationship because he "didn't like to do it" and he was "traumatized" that his ex "forced him to do it so much." After a few weeks, when I'd question why he wasn't in the mood or picking up on my sexual queues, he would tell me that we weren't sexually compatible and I was too aggressive of a kisser (which would be the first time in my life I was ever told that).

Hunter would even flirt with other girls in front of me. During one of our dates, he started chatting with this brunette girl sitting next to us at a comedy club and made a slick, flirty comment about how his "type" was women with dark hair. That's cool and all, except I was blonde at the time.

Sadly, I continued to stay because whenever we'd fight or he'd be scared I'd go away, he'd tell me that he loved me and made sure to send me a cute good morning text the next day—and everyone knows I'm a sucker for a cute good morning text.

"Plus, no one will ever care for you like I do," he'd constantly plant in my mind. *"Flaws and all."*

He did impress me—at least *outside* of our relationship. After all, he was a recovering addict who was on a path to betterment and had to fight those "itches" every moment of every day, as he described it. Instead, he funneled those urges into his work. Hunter eventually quit his gig at the barber shop and fully immersed himself into fashion by becoming a partial business partner at the clothing store.

Being the supportive girlfriend that I was—and knowing that he needed help to elevate his dreams—I stepped in a few days a week to work at the store and promote his brand. So yes, I worked my career full-time, studied my graduate classes, worked my graduate assistant-ship (this helped me pay for my MBA), and stocked and organized clothes at his shop over one hour away while principles of international marketing terms buzzed around in my head.

Knowing just how hard he had been working to build his brand, I wanted to surprise him with a deep-cleaned room. I figured that a cluttered room leads to a cluttered mind, which could deter his progress.

After all, his room was your typical bachelor pad, but to the umpteenth power. There was grime caked into his window blinds, rotted red Solo cups shagged in the corner under his bed, and sticky shot glasses that began to almost mold themselves into his disheveled drawers (where no article of clothing was actually folded). As I cleaned, I started to uncover hidden stashes of notes, pictures, and gifts from former relationships. There was even a box in his desk drawer stuffed with one of their old thongs. I questioned whether or not I was dating a serial killer with all of these "trophies." (Flashbacks of the show *Dexter* looped in my mind as Michael C. Hall's character collected blood samples from each of his victims.) I feverishly texted my friends asking for advice. They told me to leave his "bum ass" behind because that was "seriously sociopathic." I wanted to agree, but I didn't want to necessarily *believe* it. Instead, I questioned him, and he agitatedly responded, *"I didn't know it was there. It's not a big fucking deal, Bri."*

I never fully trusted him after that point. As such, our days once filled with laughter and lighthearted jokes swiftly transitioned into a fleet of daily arguments. There'd be times that he'd continue to tell me that he simply couldn't talk to me for days on end because he was "too busy." Or even instances when he wouldn't have sex with me at all anymore because he just "wasn't in the mood" or "turned on." There was even that one time I was getting ready to hop in the shower and he sternly looked my naked physique up and down as he condescendingly told me that my body wasn't ideal. (In fact, his exact words were: *"Let's face it, you're not the best looking without clothes on."*).

In the hopes that Hunter could perhaps speak to me with a bit more kindness, a few weeks later while we were driving around and talking about our childhoods I felt this sudden urge to relieve myself of the weight of forever hiding onto this one pivotal (and painful) experience. In fact, I always questioned whether or not I was doing myself—and others in my life—a massive disservice by not sharing such an integral wound. Despite his attacks that forever aimed at my vulnerabilities, I somehow convinced myself that if I disclosed my deepest secret, perhaps I could tap into a more compassionate layer within him.

"Hunter, I kinda want to share with you something that I've kept hidden from everyone in my life," I gently said. *"Maybe knowing this part of me will, well, bring us closer somehow."*

"What are you talking about?" he confusedly responded.

I reiterated my upbringing with an absent father, facing years of bullying, and being manipulated by men—but then I mentioned the worst offender of them all.

"This isn't the easiest thing to really say," I whispered as I tried to hold back tears. *"And I'm sorry for getting emotional… I've just, uh, never vocalized this before."*

"What are you talking about, Brianna?" he once again questioned. *"Can you spit it out?"*

"I...," I said with a deep pause, *"was sexually abused when I was in elementary school."*

While growing up, my home always had this open invitation style for families, friends, and neighbors in need. It was practically a "rest stop" for those trying to get back on their feet. Being that our family came from very little in terms of finances, we created this micro-community that looked out for others whenever possible. So in the third grade, when Arnold, a close family friend, was released from jail after having been sentenced for drug distribution and trafficking with no place to go, my family welcomed him with open arms. He first stayed at my aunt's house and then shifted to my home in order to live a bit closer to his HVAC job. This way, as it was explained to me, he could save enough money to finally be equipped to rent a place of his own after a few weeks or months.

"Never deprive someone of help if you can give it," my Mema would reinforce growing up.

Arnold was probably in his early- to mid-thirties and was relatively tall. (Well, to be fair, at a third-grade height everyone looked quite massive from that perspective.) He had a thick, black beard and typically wore a variety of black and navy-blue Yankees baseball caps. His upper extremities were covered with black and white prison-style tattoos. Despite his "rougher" physical appearance, he appeared quite calm, polite, and charming in his demeanor. I mean, who else would volunteer to play dress-up with my Barbie dolls and really get into character? He would even lob wiffle balls my way in the backyard as I swung (and typically missed), pretend to eat the plastic food that I'd create on my play kitchen stove, and even help me organize my bookshelf. We quickly became the best of buddies.

After a few weeks, though, he became a bit too friendly.

The typical school morning routine consisted of my mom waking up relatively early to pack my lunch and take care of my brother while my stepdad would have already gone to work at that point. My alarm clock would start buzzing at around 6:50 a.m., which would signal for me to go shower. My tiny little feet would patter on over to the bathroom where I'd shut the door, undress, and enter the shower through the sliding patterned glass privacy door. I'd be in there for several minutes as I'd bathe and dance to a Britney Spears song in my head and get ready like a *"good, big girl,"* as my mom always smiled and said to me.

On one particular morning, though, my routine was disrupted. After I turned the water nozzle on and stepped into the shower, I heard the knob to the bathroom door slowly turn. Arnold peeked behind the door frame and crept into my space.

"Shhhhh," he said as I fearfully made eye contact with him. *"It's just me, don't worry. Don't let me disturb you."*

I sat there in silence for a few seconds as the stream of water pounded over my head and fell to the shower floor.

"It's just me," he said as he softly closed the door. *"I just need to use the bathroom. Pretend I'm not even here."*

I immediately remember feeling uncomfortable despite my age and never having been formally exposed to the basic school principles of "sexual education." I instinctively started to crouch down into a ball to hide from Arnold's line of sight in the far-left corner of the shower. Although the glass pattern slightly distorted the crisp image of me within the ceramic-tiled walls, Arnold was still able to see the basic shapes of my body as he made his way over to the toilet, dropped his pants, and appeared to urinate. When I didn't hear any liquid hit the toilet bowl water and instead heard grunts as he rubbed his hands up and down his private area, this further solidified that something was *off*. At first, he massaged himself slowly as he smirked over at me while I continued to try and hide my naked body with my loofah. He progressively increased the jerking motion over the next few minutes until he seemed to finally relieve himself directly into the toilet—which caused my entire body to cringe.

"Make sure to flush before you leave," he instructed. Without any further conversation, Arnold then pulled his pants up and slowly walked out of the bathroom.

For the next two weeks, Arnold would interrupt my morning routine and violate my peace for the sake of his own self-pleasure. During the third week, he actually started to open my shower door to get a "better look" at me.

"I just want to make sure that you're getting clean in all the right places," he muffled under his breath.

He'd proceed to stare at me as I again tried to cover my body from his devilish eyes. The more scared I grew, the more gratification he seemed to derive. Once he fully captured the image of me that he wanted, he'd leave the shower door slightly open, waltz on over to the toilet, and commence his groans. I'd scrunch myself over in an attempt to cover my chest and legs, shuffle over to the door, and close it so that I didn't have to watch him in high-definition. As these morning rituals progressed, this level of dirtiness accumulated within me despite these having occurred during my bathing hours.

Growing scared each day that Arnold might try to physically touch me, one morning I decided to lock the bathroom door. As expected, when he tried to enter the bathroom, I heard him furiously twist the doorknob back-and-forth in an effort to "unjam" it. Recognizing that I have grown aware of his actions, Arnold let out a heavy grunt and presumably went back to the guest bedroom. For the next week to follow, Arnold would try to push his luck and jiggle the handle to see if my locking was only a one-off occurrence. To his dismay, I proceeded to develop a lifelong habit of forever locking the bathroom door—even if I was only brushing my teeth.

Though our bathroom interactions ceased to exist past that point, Arnold would still try and play—especially while my mom and stepdad were doing chores. There was one time while my mom was in the living room hanging up pictures and my stepdad was out back doing yard work that Arnold was entertaining my brother and me on the other side of the house by tossing a plush football around. He'd throw us passes and encourage us to run down the hallway to complete a touchdown.

After having caught one of his passes and sprinting with all of my might toward the end of the hallway, Arnold said, *"And here comes the tackle!"* as he then swept me up, threw me over his arms, and then gently tackled me to the ground.

After precisely placing me on my back, Arnold then hopped on top of me in a plank-like position and pinned my wrists to the ground. He looked at me with those devilish eyes again and held his position for a few seconds before he muttered, *"This is what it feels like when there's no pressure."*

I was confused as Arnold then pushed his pelvic area directly on top of my lower abdomen. *"And this is what it feels like when there IS pressure,"* he continued. *"Do you feel the difference?"* he added as he aggressively stabbed me through his jeans with his erect penis. Every time thereafter that he'd be making contact with me, he'd reinforce that this is what "pressure" felt like.

I didn't respond—and for the next two minutes I wildly tried to free myself from his grip as he dry-humped me.

"Please stop!" I finally cried.

Once he finally released his restraint, I sprinted over to my mom in the living room and latched onto her. *"What's wrong, Bri?"* my mom questioned.

I wanted to say that Arnold was scaring me, but then he walked in from the hallway and flashed me this look of frustration as if he was telling me, *"Don't you dare say a word."*

"Nothing, mom," I said, frightened. *"I'm just hungry."*

About two weeks after that roleplay, Arnold moved out after having saved enough to get his own apartment. Though I would run into him at family parties moving forward into my early adulthood, I would always try to avoid him.

"Why are you so weird around him?" Mema questioned me on one occasion.

"There's just something about him, Mema," I responded. *"I don't like him."*

As I explained this story to Hunter through my Niagara Falls-like flow of tears, Hunter seemed confused yet angry while processing this information. After a few seconds of silence, Hunter finally let out a deep breath and said, *"Why haven't you told anyone about this? Why are you telling me this now? It doesn't make sense."*

"I don't know…" I cried. *"I was scared for so many years that no one would believe me or that Arnold would somehow try and make me pay for it in another way… I really don't know. I somehow felt comfortable in this moment with you."*

"Well, I'm sorry you went through that, Brianna," Hunter said as he started to pull onto his street and alongside my car parked a few houses down, *"…but your trauma is not my trauma, and you can't use that against me."*

"Wait, what?" I said as I balled. *"Use it against you?"*

"Yeah, you can't use your crazy against me," he said.

"That's all you have to say to that?" I said in disbelief.

"I'm going to need you to get out of my car now," he said.

"You're going to kick me out after I just told you that?!" I sadly questioned. *"You're the only loved one I ever opened up to about this!"*

"Brianna, get out of my fucking car," he said. *"I need to think about all of this right now, and I need to go."*

"I just told you my deepest fucking secret and now you're going to leave me?" I sobbed.

"Get the FUCK out of my car!" he snapped.

I weakly slugged out from his car and managed to pull myself into the driver seat of my own. Once I closed my door, Hunter's car engine simultaneously revved. He quickly drove off and left me abandoned in my car for nearly an hour as I wept and contemplated my existence. This wave of depression drowned me faster than my own tears.

He's not concerned with problems that aren't his own.

RATIONALIZING THE RED FLAG: I just can't rationalize this one. Unfortunately, I shared something so personal with a man who never truly respected me. More than anything, why did I choose this moment to tell him of all people that? What did I think would change in him?

WHAT I SHOULD'VE DONE: Told my mom and the people who love me most so that I could heal, get proper support, and deal with this very real traumatizing period of my life.

I FORGIVE MYSELF FOR: Thinking he would care at all.

IF IT HAPPENS AGAIN: I would look for the signs of narcissism.

SELF-LOVE LESSON: Traumas need to be healed from within.

I would cry. Multiple times a day actually. He made me feel low—but it was to a point where I felt so belittled, worthless, and ugly that I was almost conditioned to believe that no one else would "love" me. My cries were constantly shoved down by gaslighting remarks that I was "too sensitive," that I "couldn't take a joke," or that I was "the problem."

Over time, I somehow started to believe that this attention—as negative as it was—would be all that I would get from a man. My diminished sense of self-worth then turned into isolation and depression.

My friends started to believe that similar to his exes, I, too, was fully immersed in a dysfunctional codependent relationship with Hunter. While desperately trying to grip the reins of the relationship as I felt my power slip from my fingertips, I realized that I relinquished my identity, my self-worth, and my self-respect over to him. I sacrificed my wants for him, developed this "loyal-to-a-fault" mentality, discarded my ability to properly articulate my emotions, and morphed into an unrecognizable version of myself in the hopes that he'd approve of this "me" in his mind.

Wanting to interfere, my friends insisted that they meet Hunter. Wanting to avoid embarrassment and shame, though, I would leave those inquiries unanswered for quite some time.

When I finally decided to step out for my birthday and introduce everyone to him, all he did was make comments about my weight (*"Do you really need another bite of that pizza?"* he snarked in front of Scarlett) and my "crazy embarrassing" dances. That was the ending of any future interaction Hunter had with any of my friends. My outgoing, free-spirited self who once shined so brightly now hid in the dimly lit crevices of his room. Alone. Embarrassed. Ashamed. As the weeks went by, I found myself being ambushed from every angle of his verbal and emotional attacks again. Belittled and betrayed, I truthfully started to believe that I was this innately unlovable beast that no one would ever find attractive.

My relationship with Hunter was as rocky as the mountains—and quite frankly I was getting sick of hiking. That is, until Hunter gifted me with a literal view of the Alps for Christmas with a fully paid and arranged trip to France in March. People don't do these things unless they're really in love, right? (At least that's what I told myself.)

Mathematically and financially speaking, it made sense to me. Therefore, by those calculations I determined that we were back in love.

"Hunter," I softly said as my eyes welled up with happy tears. "This is, like, a different version of you. Why are you doing and giving me all of this?"

"I realize how important you are to me and how I will do anything to show you just how much you mean to me," he reinforced.

The next few months were full of love and excitement in anticipation of our country-wide exploration into the home of some of the world's most magnificent museums, art galleries, and fine cuisines—that is, until the world started to shift as coronavirus emerged. Our dream of going to Europe was defunct as it was deemed one of the epicenters of the virus. We had to quickly shift and rebook another trip so that the credits wouldn't expire. I suggested that we venture within the United States to avoid any travel complications. He suggested Egypt. So, we "compromised" and went to Egypt. (Hey, at least it was still a getaway.)

Opinions were split as we asked if we should travel outside of the country. "It's nothing more than the flu," a few people barked. Others, though, warned that we should stay home and just "wait it out." My anxiety-riddled self wanted to just call it quits—both the trip and the relationship.

Hunter insisted that we go and insisted that it was, once again, part of a "grander plan." We packed our bags and hopped on our first plane to Morocco. Once we landed and turned our phones off from airplane mode as we made our way to the connecting flight, we were flooded with hundreds of texts from people laughing at us for now being "stuck" at the airport because the then-President announced a travel ban while we were mid-flight.

"Hunter, we need to get home!" I panicked as I noted that a one-way ticket home was priced at over $2,000 per person. "I'll charge it to my card! I don't even care at this point!"

Hunter insisted that we fly to our final stop in Cairo as we could "stay in our hotel" and "figure it out." My mom disapproved and screamed at me through the phone for thinking like a "runaway child." (If it was possible for my mom to have strangled me through a phone, I'm pretty positive I would've been choked out and lying unconscious on that airport floor as stampedes of frantic tourists stormed over me and bombarded the help desks.)

The sound of nonstop coughs echoed throughout the cabin the duration of the flight to Cairo. Hunter and I weren't equipped with masks, either. I tied one of my sweatshirts around my face and doused my hands in hand sanitizer. I'm pretty sure I got high off of the intoxicating fumes of the ethanol. A child profusely vomited eerily similar to the scene in *The Exorcist* one row behind us. It was bright orange. I genuinely thought that I was going to contract the virus and die in Egypt. Hopefully they'd bury me near some of the pharaohs, I tried to dark humor-ly tell myself.

When we arrived in Egypt, we made our way to our hotel, immediately undressed, and stood in defeat under the head of the shower as burning hot water melted our skin for nearly an hour. I hugged him and cried as what felt like streams of lava ran down my spine. I wanted to go home. I wanted to be safe—and happy.

The next morning, the gentleman at the front desk seemed to be under the predisposition that everything was functioning "as normal." In fact, he assured us that only a few of the locals decided to wear a mask in order to "make the tourists feel safe"—otherwise, it was business as usual. He recommended that we spend the day in Giza to view the Great Sphinx and Great Pyramid. We followed suit and hopped on the Metro Line 2. It only took about five minutes for the ricocheting of coughs to begin against the walls of the train car. I insisted that we go home, but Hunter wanted to "ride it out." After all, he said that we had to prove everyone at home wrong.

With each passing day that we were in Egypt, more lockdown measures were implemented. By the third day we were living solely off of bread, mashed fava beans, and grape leaves from one of the only shops that was allowed to stay open. Public transportation was shut down. Monuments and areas of interest were closed. We were confined to the streets of Cairo maskless as the virus spread. I would call Hunter's mom crying telling her that I wanted to book flights home while Hunter was sleeping—but she insisted that it would "work out."

The next day I made my way to the U.S. Embassy to figure out how we could get home—except the office was closed. Simultaneously, I received non-stop notifications from United Airlines regarding restrictions and mandates, along with updates to our return flights. I was alerted that the "transfer" airport kept shifting as more countries closed their borders. I tried calling the airline's support staff and was told that I'd be on hold for more than forty-eight hours. We had to wait it out and pray that our flight would remain. Eventually, the airline rerouted us to a layover in London and notified us through their app and several email notifications.

Thankfully we were able to fly back to the States. I again tied a sweatshirt around my face and snorted ethanol for nearly nine hours as it permeated off of my body. The layover was filled with thousands of individuals donned in what appeared to mimic Walter White's infamous meth-making costume in *Breaking Bad*. For a brief moment I thought that I was at a dystopian roleplaying convention of sorts. When individuals from the Centers for Disease Control and Prevention (CDC) made us sign formalized virus-tracking paperwork, though, I quickly snapped out of that vision.

We quarantined together at Hunter's house for several weeks while he made claims that the virus was "obviously fake" given that we didn't test positive after multiple urgent care visits. I was traumatized in these weeks, though. All I wanted to do was hug my mom and ask her to save me from this roller coaster ride from hell—but I didn't want to potentially make her sick being that we were still learning about this virus.

As we inched closer to the end of our "love nest lockdown," tensions continued to rise. Hunter was growing more irritable and restless by the minute knowing that he couldn't work. When he wasn't lashing out at me (or making fun of my "bigger left breast" or painfully cracking my knuckles despite my cries to stop), he was either screaming at the government or preaching that we all needed to get much closer to God as a country. Hunter's addiction was now being fully funneled into religion and politics.

His lullabies quickly became nothing but podcasts of his two new-found interests. The last night of my quarantine occurred when Hunter passed out to the ever-so-delicate sound of polarized reporters bickering from a background video playing on his phone. I tried tapping him awake to ask him to please shut the video off. After several failed attempts, I took his phone and tried to close out the app. In my efforts, his most recently used app popped up—which was Snapchat. Though minimized, I saw that his top notification was from one of his exes that he claimed he hasn't spoken to in years—who directly adjacent to her name was a fire emoji and the number "525" (so they have been talking for 525 consecutive days)—along with several other females with other varying Snap streaks who were sending him promiscuous messages.

I shook him out of his trance and screamed at him to explain himself. I swear that I felt *and* saw his soul leave his body knowing that he was caught. All he could muster up the courage to say was something along the lines of "*I'm sorry I lied to you*" as I threw clothes at him and cursed every profanity possible in his name. I grabbed bags from the floor and started reclaiming my belongings.

In what appeared to be part of the cycle, I sped home half-blinded by tears and fueled by rage. When I got home, I opened my phone to paragraphs of text explaining that he's "not worthy of me." He was right—but I was weak. And so, I continued to text him demanding answers while he completely shut off communication for several days to follow. (This is known as the "discarding" stage, or the point when a narcissist realizes that you will no longer fuel his ego. Here, he realized that I was asking for compromise, empathy, honesty, and boundaries—and he lacked any and all of those qualities.)

He's a habitual liar.

RATIONALIZING THE RED FLAG: It's less rationalizing and more like not knowing what's real. When somebody lies to you this much, you start to question your own reality...

WHAT I SHOULD'VE DONE: Ended things a long time ago.

I FORGIVE MYSELF FOR: Staying in a relationship way past its expiration date and questioning my own truth while enduring his lies.

IF IT HAPPENS AGAIN: I will not accept any of this.

SELF-LOVE LESSON: I cannot build a kingdom upon an unstable foundation. Ultimately, it will collapse.

Like a sick yo-yo, though, I'd come back to him through his manip-ulative tactics. He didn't *fully* discard me knowing that there was still some attention and ego-boosting left to squeeze out if he tugged hard enough. It became almost masochist in nature. I knew he would hurt me, but I ate the pain. At one point, though, I was attempting to detox from him. It's true that Hunter essentially became a drug to me. When

I was with him—whether we were fighting or not—I got a "high." Now I was crashing, withdrawing, and fearful of relapsing.

And then I did.

All it took was one text message from him professing his "love" after months apart.

What I envision a recovering addict would feel like at the sight of a line of glistening white powder, I opened my nostril and deeply inhaled Hunter back into my system.

Looking Within at Personal
RED FLAGS

- You do more for him than he does for you.

- You are entirely too giving.

- You start blaming other people for your partner's wrongdoings (such as an ex), yet your partner doesn't know how to implement healthy, respectable boundaries and make you feel secure.

- You don't use your voice to insist on the support you need to get through a tough time.

- You overlook how he speaks about other women.

- You share an intimate, vulnerable secret with a narcissist hoping that they finally show you love and compassion.

- You need a trip halfway around the world to rekindle the romance (only for it to disappear within a hot minute upon return).

- You allow yourself to continue riding on a roller coaster of a relationship.

CONTENT WARNING

This next chapter contains stories of narcissistic abuse on mental, emotional, and spiritual levels.

11

THE DOWNWARD DESCENT

Growing up I always told my mom that I wanted to be a marine biologist, but I never expected that I would metaphorically keep submerging my heart into heavily baited water as great whites continued to ram against my steel-framed rib cage. These animals would somehow break down my barriers and sink their serrated blade-like teeth into my delicate skin while feasting on my blood.

Inwardly, I felt like chum—and these predators smelled that from miles away.

Especially Hunter.

Eventually, though, I convinced myself into believing that for us to remain in contact despite the damage, there must've been some form of divine energy between us. Maybe we were that couple that had to knock out all of the hardships in the beginning to finally smooth the waters for sailing.

These were comical thoughts to my friends, though, who at this point wanted to strip me of my wetsuit and instead plop me into a clown outfit so that they could then squeak my nose and clap as I twist together a zoo of balloon animals.

After all, Hunter started to cancel cuddle sessions in replacement of religious, political, and survivalistic extracurriculars. Hunter started to build a bunker, stock up on end-of-the-world supplies, and withdraw his entire life savings from the bank in fear of the financial system collapsing. These beliefs were amplified with every passing event that he'd frequent.

Hunter started traveling to cities all across the country on the weekends to attend religious rallies and political protests, so he would leave me for days. During one of the late-night events, he sent me videos of hordes of people with conflicting ideologies fighting on the streets. One scene in particular was filled with shrieks of people yelling to *"RUN BACK TO THE HOTEL!"* and white noise of constant coughing from what appeared to be an infiltration of smoke bombs and bear mace. In one of the clips, I even somehow heard a woman fearfully howl, *"Hunter! Hunter, HELP!"* (I'm not happy to admit that I must've replayed that video dozens of times.) I asked him who that was—and he completely ignored me.

With suspicions raised, I started looking on his pages for some "leads." Instead, though, I discovered Hunter's hidden Parler account (an alternative social networking site). He was not only liking pictures of half-naked women as American flag bikini tops hoisted up their perfectly sculpted breasts, but he was engaging in conversations with ones who tagged their locations as being in cities that he would be visiting. I guess he was so infatuated with one female's pose that he lost his ability to formulate words and relied on our modern-day hieroglyphics by commenting the following emojis in sequential order: gasping mouth, American flag, heart eye face, and fire. Even the ancient Egyptians would have encouraged a bit more creativity.

I tried calling Hunter to discuss this, but he insisted that he was so devastated by "the sins" he had witnessed that he needed to go to sleep. When I then lost my composure questioning the use of his Parler account, he told me that he "could do whatever" since it wasn't "a big deal" because "all men do it." The disrespect and hypocrisy continued to accumulate.

Distraught by the civil unrest being spread even faster than the virus around the nation, Hunter set out on another mission: to organize his own religious and political movement of like-minded individuals who "wanted to *un*-separate the church from state." Most people he met at prior events, some from Parler, and a few via secret Facebook groups. They would meet at various undisclosed locations to discuss ways to "defend" themselves against a "rapture-like occurrence," purchase plots of land to build a "community hideout," and program their ham radios to dial-in on the same frequency in fear of a "blackout." The goal was to create a localized group that they could depend on since there's "power in numbers." Hunter's vision was to then branch this into chapters on a national scale. I saw a hunger in him for power that genuinely intimidated me—but the more that I heard him talk, the more fearful I grew that he *very well* may be right about the world pretty much ending or a bloodbath of a civil war being on the horizon.

As more people turned to him for leadership, Hunter's power trip amplified. He quickly started to create a constitution for this group, which included sections on oaths, values, roles, responsibilities, meetings, codes of conduct, and dress codes (which entailed camo tactical pants, work boots, and solid-colored tank tops bearing the group's logo). Somehow, I found myself editing this document line-by-line since "I'm a writer" and "that's what I'm good for." I felt like I was a victim of emotional kidnapping, and I developed Stockholm syndrome.

Essentially, it felt like this man wanted to play chess, and I falsely convinced myself that I could channel the skills of Beth Harmon from *The Queen's Gambit*. I declared checkmate as the holidays approached.

For Christmas—which was a distraction to his "patriotic and religious" efforts—Hunter oh-so-thoughtfully purchased my main present at Cabela's, a premium outdoor gear and sporting goods store. It was a weekend trip to explore the Ozark Mountains in Arkansas that I'm convinced was some kind of sign-up bonus that he received after applying for a store credit card. He also spent the morning of Christmas Eve cherry-picking last minute items for me at the mall, which included socks and an unflattering puffer jacket that made me look like I was auditioning to be a backup dancer in Missy Elliot's "The Rain" music video. (Now that I think about it, though, that and my M.C. Hammer pants might make for one hell of an outfit.)

When I got a bit teary-eyed after opening presents because I felt like his gifts weren't personal, he looked at me with disdain and told me that I was "the most ungrateful woman" he'd ever been with.

When the word "party" in the lyrics *"It's my party and I'll cry if I want to"* can be easily interchanged with any other noun (such as holiday, birthday, or even just a Monday…), I recognized that I was miserable. I was crying every single day over slick comments and actions toward me that made me feel inferior. This was no longer love. In fact, I'm not sure it ever actually was. Instead, I started to dabble with the idea that it was an attachment that I had developed out of a deep-rooted yearning to feel loved by a man romantically. The more serious problem at-hand, though, was that I was stuck in a soul-sucking black hole: the more broken that Hunter made me feel, the more worthless I felt as a person, which then translated into a greater need for validation from the only depleting source that I had at the moment: Hunter. I couldn't escape. I felt like I was trapped in a vacuum-sealed package as every ounce of my being was being drained.

One week later was New Year's Eve. I was invited to go over to my best friend's house. Hunter resisted. Knowing that I was going to see my friends out of tradition, Hunter instead decided to throw his own party with members of his organization. I decided to go to my friend's for the first half of the night while staying entirely sober, driving nearly two hours, and then surprising Hunter just in time for the ball drop so we could kiss and welcome in the new year with new vibes. I arrived several minutes shy of midnight. Once the ball dropped, Hunter welcomed in the new year by whipping out his phone, recording the television, and then panning across the room as other couples kissed. I guess our "new year" didn't officially start until 12:07 a.m. when he finally decided to come sluggishly kiss me.

The real holiday that Hunter couldn't wait to celebrate was an upcoming rally out in the western half of the U.S. to protest the country's current lockdown measures, vaccine mandates, and voting system. He ordered that everyone dress in code and march in unison while members held a variety of police shields to "show-off the group on a larger scale."

"Is this all really necessary?" I questioned. *"This doesn't feel right, Hunter."*

"The same thing could've been said about the Crusades," he smirked. *"But you fight for what you rightfully believe in."*

One individual was even instructed to parade around the streets bearing a massive flagpole that showcased the group's logo. Every ounce of my being didn't want to go to this event (it was my first and last)— but I was terrified of not seeing Hunter for a few days as he practically camped out. (It's sad to admit that I was more fixated on Hunter potentially finding love in the streets with a woman as religiously-driven and American-flag-adorned as he was than I was with my own conscience and values.)

A group of about forty individuals all met up at a park in Philly that Hunter designated as the "meet-up" at around 2 a.m. and created a caravan. At one of the rest stops, we met several other "like-minded" groups. Hunter talked with them, told them of the group's mission, and recruited dozens of other cars along the way.

After nearly two days of driving, we arrived at the hotel where it was arranged so that we basically occupied one entire floor. We unloaded our bags and met in the suite to discuss the "operations" for the day. One member had a map of all of the streets that we were to march down. Another member programmed walkie talkies so that we could communicate if the cell towers were to crash. There was also the individual whose mission was to distribute kubotons (basically aluminum self-defense keychains) to all of the females "in case things got rowdy." Hunter then told us to get dressed and meet outside of the hotel lobby.

Fearful of risking my identity (and honestly even just going in general), I ensured that I concealed every distinguishable mark of my body. Band-Aids masked my tattoos, gloves covered my detectable acrylic nails, glasses shielded my eyes, a hat hid my forehead, and a neck gaiter removed any other potential exposure of my facial characteristics. I wore several layers of clothing, too, to distort the curvature of my body.

And so, we marched. Within moments of us leaving the hotel, a group of individuals wearing all black sprayed an entire can of bear mace at our group and set-off several smoke bombs. My eyes immediately started tearing as I tried to hold my breath from what I imagined could only be poison. I quickly became disoriented as I tried to meander through this thick, suffocating cloud. While gasping for air, refraining from scratching out my rapidly burning eyes, and barely finding my bearings, I somehow used my adrenaline to propel me as far away from that scene as possible. I only stopped running when, in the distance, I heard Hunter screaming, *"Get him!"* Apparently, a knife was pulled by one of these individuals. Several of Hunter's men broke the cloud and started beating the guy down. A police officer came over and stopped the mayhem.

**He's impacting the way that you
behave and who you are becoming.**

RATIONALIZING THE RED FLAG: *"I don't trust being with him,
and I don't trust being without him... but I'd rather be with him
than be alone with nothing but my chaotic, self-deprecating
thoughts."*

WHAT I SHOULD'VE DONE: Realized that this wasn't me in
terms of my values, ideals, or beliefs. (This is especially true
when it comes to my political philosophies: I'm more of a
"purple" person as opposed to a die-hard "blue" or a "red" as I
genuinely side with either of the two parties depending on the
topic at-hand.) But again this... this wasn't me at all.

I FORGIVE MYSELF FOR: Staying in a relationship that not only
damaged the trust that I had in myself, but also in the way that
I viewed the world—both within me and around me.

IF IT HAPPENS AGAIN: I won't seek another relationship until I
fully solidify my own self-love and firmly establish my values.
Having a healthy, secure view of myself can reduce the risk of
potentially entertaining another toxic individual—who could
very well change me and, if I'm not careful enough, could even
make me become toxic, too.

SELF-LOVE LESSON: I must invest in my own self-esteem so
that no relationship could ever separate me from my authentic
sense of self.

Once the smoke dissipated, several individuals went upstairs to
wash their eyes out with water and milk. Someone actually thought
ahead and packed anti-bear mace wipes that would help to alleviate
the everlasting burning sensation. (I didn't even know a product like
that existed.) The smell was so pungent that some of the members had
to actually throw out their clothes and change.

I didn't realize the magnitude of what I had just gotten myself into—and I began to panic knowing that I was practically alone in another state. I quickly sent a text to one best friend letting her know my whereabouts *just* in case. She wasn't proud of my decision in the least, but she appreciated my transparency and ensured that she would communicate with my family about my location, if needed.

Where we were exactly headed I had absolutely no idea, but we seemed to just follow the masses. I felt like I was in the movie *Z Day*—except the zombies were religious and freedom fighters just piling onto the other in the name of patriotism and prayer. Groans about the First Amendment were the ways in which these beings communicated, and I was terrified they were going to sniff me out as fresh, independent blood. The environment felt extreme—and let's be honest, Charles Darwin hasn't equipped our kind to survive in such conditions.

The more that we marched, the more individuals that started to flood in. The force from one of the surges acted like a riptide as it dragged me away from Hunter and the rest of the group. Now completely separated with no functioning phone signal, I felt like I was drowning in the middle of a tight, moveless (nearly vacuum-sealed) crowd as I tried to slowly finagle my way out. Panic ensued as each person practically pinned me to my position like some form of seaweed that wrapped around my extremities and chained me down as the tide continued to rise.

It took me about two hours to finally break from the crowd. Somehow, I spotted a person waving around the group's flag about one mile away, so I sprinted toward the individual in the hopes that Hunter was nearby.

"Hey! HEY!" I managed to scream as I waved my hands at the member to get his attention. *"Do you know where Hunter is?"*

"I have no idea where anyone is," he said. *"That huge crowd came in, everyone was separated and then a few people spotted a group of people attacking us freedom fighters and they went to go give 'em the business."*

"Do you know if Hunter was there?" I panicked.

"I'm not sure, but I'll help you find him and hopefully some of the others," he responded.

Like a detective trying to look for leads, I figured that we should make our ways to areas in the city that seemed a bit more "chaotic" or that appeared to have more police activity. Though cautious, I assumed that if fighting was involved, Hunter would more than likely be in or around the situation. I walked for nearly thirty minutes when I finally saw a pack of group members exhaustingly approach us from the other side of the block.

"HUNTER!?" I screamed. *"Is that you?"*

"Yes, it's me," he said. As I approached him, he appeared to be soaked in sweat although the temperature was below freezing.

"Where were you guys?!" I frantically questioned. *"What happened to you and everyone, and why do you all look so disheveled?"*

"We were just doing what we set out to do," he smirked as he looked back at his other members. *"We made sure our people were safe and then handled the situation when needed."* The group madly laughed behind him as excess testosterone seemed to diffuse from their pores.

"Can we go back to the hotel now, please?" I begged.

"I'm not heading back anytime soon," he sternly stated. *"I came here for a mission, and I will fulfill it until we drive back home."*

"I'm scared, Hunter… please," I said. *"This is dangerous, and I don't want anyone to get hurt."*

"This is why I didn't want you to come to these things in the first place," he snapped. *"I knew you'd get like this, but I didn't want you to bitch and complain from home, either."*

"Hunter… please, just come back with me for a little bit so we can talk about this and come back to reality," I sadly said.

"I'll meet you in the room later," he said as he shifted his attention toward answering an "incoming transmission" on his walkie talkie

about a brawl several blocks away. *"I have to go, but I'll have one of the guys walk you back to the hotel safely."*

"You're going to leave me?" I questioned as my eyes started to tear.

"Duty calls," he said as he then instructed his group to march past me toward the new location.

I was escorted back to the hotel room in mental silence despite the chants, yells, and fights that surrounded me. Hunter not only dismissed my concerns and embarrassed me in front of his guys, but he chose to pursue religion and politics (or whatever you want to call this) over his "person." As I was relieved of my personal bodyguard once I entered the hotel, I dismally walked up toward my room on the fourth floor. Upon entering, I shut and locked the door, leaned against the bathroom wall, and slid down it as I sobbed and crashed on my butt.

"Why am I HERE?!" I cried aloud. *"What am I DOING?!"*

Overwhelmed with emotions, I decided to shower and crawl into the bed as I surrounded myself with a warm cocoon of hotel blankets. I fell asleep after having waited three hours for Hunter's return. I bombarded him with texts and all he'd sporadically respond with is that he'd *"be back soon."* He didn't come back until around 3 a.m.

Watching his personality shift so abruptly and drastically around this group didn't sit well with me. In fact, his overall presence in my life started to manifest into physical sickness. I felt dependent on him as if he held my antidote, though.

Except I knew I needed to get away.

I went nearly one month without speaking to Hunter after that point in an attempt to break the "trauma bond," or the connection an abused person feels toward the abuser. I almost received my thirty days "clean" key tag—similar to an AA meeting except it was for my celebration of "no contact"—until I received a text message from a random number: *"Hey, Bri… I just wanted to say that I am really proud of you."*

"Hey, who is this?" I naively responded.

"I'm sorry for everything and I miss you," he texted me one day. *"I really want to see you."*

I felt like I somehow swallowed my heart at the thought of seeing him after so long—though understanding that's not anatomically possible.

Convinced that in-person closure would alleviate my pain, I obliged to meet him at a sushi restaurant at a halfway point between our houses. Though irrational, if I felt like crying I presumed that I would just shove another spicy crab roll down my throat to plug up the tear ducts (although not anatomically accurate.)

Hunter arrived earlier than I did, so as I peered into the restaurant scoping out the potential booth that he snagged, I lost my breath at the sight of him in a suit staring back at me while I glanced his way. It was as if the ghost of a defensive back had just brutally tackled me at the walkway of this restaurant and depleted all air from my lungs. I shook this anxiety-riddled thought from my body, inhaled a deep breath, and walked his way. As I approached the table, Hunter stood up and greeted me with a hug.

"Hey, Bri," he said as he then gently squeezed me for several long seconds.

Once we both loosened our grips and backed away, we slowly shuffled into our respective sides of the booth while we locked eyes. Small talk proceeded as we asked those basic, awkward filler questions:

- So what's new?
- What's going on with work?
- How's your family?
- Has anything exciting happened lately?

Though the restaurant closed earlier than anticipated after having not properly updated their hours online, I learned that during our "break" Hunter had connected with a group that fundraises for certain political candidates in Pennsylvania. After having frequented events with this individual and exchanging ideologies, Hunter was asked to be a part of this team.

"I practically have an event every night now," Hunter said.

"I was wondering what was up with the suit," I responded.

"Call me crazy, but I have a feeling I can change the world," he smiled as he adjusted his cufflink and then signed for the dinner bill.

Cut short from conversation, I somehow found myself walking toward Hunter's car in the restaurant's parking lot. Before I hopped in to begin our deep dive of a dialogue, he met me at his passenger door.

"Can I have one more hug?" he questioned.

"I... I don't know if that's a good idea," I hesitantly responded.

He then opened his arms and motioned with his hands for me to come close.

"Please, Bri," he said as he invited me into his chest.

Intoxicated by his pheromones, I inched my body into his and stayed within his embrace for nearly one full minute as we slowly rocked back and forth in the cool night breeze. When I started motioning toward backing away, he pulled his head up from where it rested on my shoulder, looked down into my eyes, and then slowly fixated towards my lips.

"I can't do this," I said.

"Do what?" he smirked as he moved his mouth closer to mine in a teasing fashion.

"That," I subtly replied.

"Oh, you mean this?" he said as he then started passionately kissing me and placed his burly palms against my cheeks.

He uses physical touch to lure you back in.

RATIONALIZING THE RED FLAG: *"If my physical body isn't rejecting him... and is still attracted to him... then there HAS to still be something there between us that's worth saving, right?"*

WHAT I SHOULD'VE DONE: Realized that this was a tactic to keep me hooked.

I FORGIVE MYSELF FOR: Letting my walls down and letting him back in.

IF IT HAPPENS AGAIN: I will not let my sex drive accelerate the situation any further.

SELF-LOVE LESSON: Hooking up with someone that I'm on the rocks with will never solve the issue at-hand. Sex will provide a temporary bandage, but the wound will still need healing.

The fireworks I felt for him toward the beginning of our relationship were being set off again as if my body was celebrating an early Independence Day despite all of the accumulated trauma.

How could this be? I thought to myself.

He opened the passenger door so that I could scooch inside. Hunter walked in a semi-circumference around the front side of his car, approached the driver side, and then entered. Now inches apart from one another only separated by a middle console, I said, *"Alright, you have my attention. Go ahead and talk."*

Speaking with his nonverbal gestures, Hunter pulled my body into his so that our souls practically tangoed. We kissed, licked, and sucked the sides of the other's necks as the moonlight provided a romantic ambiance. *"God, I missed you,"* he moaned as he started nibbling on my earlobe.

"This is so bad, but so good," I moaned.

"Fuuuuuck I want to taste you," he seductively said.

"Then do it," I affirmed.

"Don't play with me, I'll go buy a room right now," he curiously said.

"Then do it," I repeated.

Hunter reached into his back pocket, whipped out his phone, and inserted "hotels near me" into his Google search bar. A nearby Hilton immediately popped up with a nightly rate of $189. Without hesitation, Hunter typed in his credit card information to finalize the reservation, turned his keys into the ignition, and started driving toward the location.

Once we arrived at the Hilton, we booked it to the check-in desk and eagerly made our way up to the king suite. As the door to our room closed, I dragged him by his tie, threw him on the bed, and ripped his belt off. I then took his pants off with my teeth as he simultaneously freed himself from his suit jacket and whipped it across the room. Though I fully wanted to take control, Hunter then tossed me onto the bed, stripped me of my clothing, and threw open my legs as he ate me for dessert. His tongue swirled around my perineal area and caused my body to shake like the epicenter of an earthquake. He took me to the point of near-orgasm until I squirmed my body out from underneath his to reciprocate the sensations.

Now laid on his back, my tongue followed the beads of sweat dripping from his chest down to his groin. I was thirsty, and he was quenching me. I also used this as lubrication as my tongue pole danced around his shaft. His moans fueled me—and mine energized him. Thus, for nearly one full hour we proceeded to exchange this control of power as we flawlessly executed every position in the Kama Sutra like pornstars.

After climaxing at the same time while passionately locking lips, we fell into the duvet covers and slept tangled within one another's naked bodies. The following morning as we both dressed and headed out to grab breakfast, I looked over at him and said, *"What… what does all of this mean?"*

"*Brianna, I don't know,*" he said as he knotted his tie around his neck. "*Why must you always question everything?*"

"*I just don't know what to think or feel,*" I said. "*That was so fucking hot and romantic, and yet here we are the next morning just pretending nothing happened.*"

"*Can't you just shut up and go to breakfast?*" he questioned. "*But not if you're going to interrogate me or cry.*"

We quickly fell back into the cycle of intense fighting. While I would question our relationship status and bicker over his obsession with religion and politics, he would bite back that I was overbearing and controlling. Our communication channels were constantly being broken, which created this distance over the next few weeks. At one point, our conversations became so foreign it was as if I were speaking French and he was speaking Arabic—and neither of us would attempt to partner with the Rosetta Stone to translate the other's needs. Instead, frustrated by the misunderstanding, he would yell at me on the phone and call me a "crazy bitch" while I would scream back out of reactive abuse that he was "the worst kind of man to exist."

"*I can't do this anymore,*" I finally texted him after our eighth screaming match via phone by 9 a.m. one morning nearly four weeks after our hotel rendezvous. "*I'm once again entirely drained, and this is killing the both of us.*"

"*Yeah… I agree,*" he said. "*I think we should meet up later, give each other that final closure, and amicably part.*"

"*How many fucking final closures do we need?*" I snarkily questioned. (Apparently, as a nod to *Mean Girls*, the limit does not exist.)

While reading that text, though, a sudden pain jolted down the side of my abdomen. It felt similar to a cramp, but different in terms of pressure and pain. I hunched over as I grabbed my stomach and said to myself, "*This motherfucker is making me sick again.*"

He knows you're a deep thinker, yet he questions you about it and gives you ultimatums.

RATIONALIZING THE RED FLAG: *"I do overthink a lot... maybe he has a point."*

WHAT I SHOULD'VE DONE: Somehow go back in time and refrain from entering that hotel with him.

I FORGIVE MYSELF FOR: Letting my body take over. Hot sex is not worth this feeling.

IF IT HAPPENS AGAIN: Another time? I think not. I can't keep doing this.

SELF-LOVE LESSON: Ultimatums are a lose-lose situation. I will choose to love myself more instead of falling into those traps.

Then I realized that I was supposed to be getting my period. Five days ago. *"Odd?"* I said aloud. *"I'm always on time with my pill pack."*

Throughout the course of that day, the pain intensified while my breasts grew tender and swollen. *"What the fuck kind of new birth control is this?"* I texted Luella.

"Girl," she said. *"I don't want to make you nervous, but have you ever considered taking a pregnancy test just to be sure?"*

"You're bugging out," I said. *"There's no way."*

Except now I couldn't shake the thought of this possibility. As I reflected on our hotel stay, I remember jokingly thinking to myself that we had just had "baby-making sex." You know, a sex so good that it'd almost be a disservice to not have his sperm and my egg meet up and high-five, but then turn around and swim away. As I ran to my nearest Walgreens to pick up two pregnancy tests, I reminded myself that I had just started a new pack of birth control pills that week. I also remembered my one OB/GYN telling me years ago that I had been diagnosed with polycystic ovary syndrome (PCOS) which could potentially cause infertility based on my various test results. (In fact, I was instructed to start taking birth control in order to "regulate" me after not having had a period for six months prior to that office visit.)

"Hopefully it's just all of the fighting and stress that's causing this," I texted Luella as I chugged a water bottle in my kitchen to make myself have to urinate.

"Either way, clearly he's impacting your body," she said. *"You need to open your eyes and stop opening your heart... and legs... to him."*

I forced my body to pee on that stick like it had just been stung by a lethal jellyfish and my urine held the remedy. As I squatted on that toilet bowl for the next seven minutes watching the lines form in the blank gray rectangular area, I prayed to a higher power that I was simply overreacting.

I realized that my egg and his sperm did more than just high-five once I saw the positive result.

Speechless, I ripped open the second test and impatiently waited as that, too, showed that I was pregnant.

I ran back to my local Walgreens and purchased three more packs of pregnancy tests along with two gallon jugs of water. After rushing home, I jolted up the stairs to my bathroom and took the next pregnancy test. And then another one. And another one. (Yes, it was the worst DJ Khaled song of all time on repeat.) I threw each of the test results on my white-tiled bathroom floor as I flung my head backwards against my bathroom wall and hysterically cried while my pants and underwear wrapped around my ankles.

I texted the picture of my positive test over to Luella and called her with a flood of tears. *"I.. do-...don't know... what to.. do!"* I managed to say through my snot-clogged nose.

"Okay, okay, let's think about this," she said. *"Have you told Hunter yet?"*

"No," I cried. *"I can't believe this… I was told this would never happen."*

"Do you want me to come over and talk?" she questioned. *"Or do you want to maybe reach out to Hunter?"*

"I… I think I should reach out to him," I sobbed. *"I just don't know how or what to say."*

I sent Hunter a text while he was at work that read: *"Hey, we need to talk about something important."*

"I'm at work, Bri, you know this and I don't have time," he responded.

"It's really something we need to talk about," I texted. I then called him, and he hit the "ignore" button.

"Bri, it needs to wait until later," he asserted.

I then sent him a picture of the pregnancy test. *"We need to talk now,"* I demanded.

It took Hunter two elongated hours to leave work before we met up in the parking lot of my local mall later that night. *"I'm freaking out, so you really need to speed this up,"* I reached out to him and said.

"I'm trying my best to leave, Bri, get off my fucking back," he said.

"This is more important than your fucking work right now," I snapped. *"Your team can handle a few fucking guests as they shop for fucking clothes."*

I waited for him in the parking lot as a Dave & Buster's sign illuminated behind me and cast a silhouette of my head against my dashboard. Once I saw him whip into his spot, he gestured for me to come into his car. I opened his door and practically wilted into his car seat as a barrage of tears sabotaged my ability to talk. Hunter placed his hand over my belly as he tried to comfort me with a slight smile.

"What are we going to do?" I questioned.

"Bri, I'll do whatever I can to help this baby," he said. *"But you know we need to keep this… that'd go against my beliefs."*

"But all we do is fight!" I cried. *"And we'd bring this baby up in the most hostile of situations… that'd kill me."*

"I'd put that all behind us to help raise this child," he said. *"I always wanted to be a father,"* he added as he peered down at my stomach.

"We don't even live together," I sobbed. *"We ourselves aren't even together! What the fuck are we?"*

"You are NOT going to use this baby as a ploy to get back together!" he yelled.

"That's not what the fuck I AM SAYING, HUNTER!" I half-screamed, half-cried. *"We practically hate each other."*

"It's this attitude that made my friend say that you're trying to trap me with this baby," he snapped.

He ignores the severity of dire situations.

RATIONALIZING THE RED FLAG: *"Maybe I'm the one at fault for breaking my 'no contact' with him… and maybe I need to keep in mind how he's feeling with this news."*

WHAT I SHOULD'VE DONE: Left him a while ago—all of these red flags are proof enough that he's not the one for me.

I FORGIVE MYSELF FOR: Getting myself into this highly-emotional and tumultuous situation.

IF IT HAPPENS AGAIN: I will not engage with someone who isn't good for me, nonetheless sleep with him (and without protection).

SELF-LOVE LESSON: Trust the truth that I know in my heart. If something feels less than loving, there is a that reason my gut is telling me to run.

"You already told your friends?!" I barked.

"Oh, like you didn't?" he said as his voice grew louder.

"Only one," I said. *"And why the fuck would I trap YOU?"*

"Because we all know that you're fucking crazy, Bri," he said. *"I was trying to be a good person here and help and here you are once again bringing out this terrible side of me."*

"Always me, Hunter... got it," I said as I cried. *"I can't fucking do this."*

We sat in silence for the next few minutes as we stared into the desolate parking lot ahead of us. Once both of our temperaments seemed to settle, I opened up the discussion by stating, *"Hunter, when you're not at the shop, which sucks up all of your time, you're now filling your few remaining gaps by helping out with some campaign. How are you possibly going to have the time to raise a baby?"*

"I mean, my mom and dad would definitely help," he said as he smirked. *"Is it sick I'm kind of excited? If it's a boy, it has to be a Hunter, Jr."*

The way that his personality and outlook on this pregnancy had shifted so suddenly induced an indescribable sense of panic into my body.

"Hunter... we are two fucked up individuals together, and I feel like we aren't ready to bring a child into this world," I gently wept.

"Why the fuck are you always crying and so overly emotional?" he said as he frustratedly looked into my eyes. *"You're a giant fucking baby, always."*

What I always anticipated would have been a moment filled with the happiest of tears in announcing a first-time pregnancy was now possessed by feelings of shame, fear, and confusion.

"Listen, we're going to keep it and do everything we can," he firmly stated. *"Go home and get some sleep, and you'll hear from me."*

Hunter plainly texted me for the next few days and focused solely on the pregnancy. Any further conversation regarding our relationship status, living conditions, or personal lives was completely neglected and ignored on his end.

"Hunter, I don't feel good," I texted him about one week later.

"What's wrong NOW, Brianna?" he downplayed.

"I'm bleeding… a lot… and I have cramps that leave me squeezing my stomach while being bedridden for hours," I said. *"I just really wish you were here with me to help."*

"You know I'm busy, Brianna, and I can get there when I can," he texted me as he then uploaded a Snapchat of him at some event for his candidate moments later.

I assumed that the emotional duress caused me to completely stain my white bed sheets that night with a puddle of blood surrounding my lower abdominal area. As I went to the bathroom to wash myself up, though, and noticed squishy, clot-like substances stuck to the bottom of my panties, I immediately called my OB/GYN. After having described my symptoms, she advised me to urgently head to the nearest emergency room.

Knowing that the hospital visitation policy restricted any loved ones from accompanying patients, I told Hunter to meet me there at the time of my arrival so that I could beg the intake nurse to allow him in for "emotional support." When she visibly noticed how high both my blood pressure and depression levels were, she granted me the ability to "sneak" Hunter into the room with me.

While I expected Hunter to be grateful for being able to understand firsthand the complications of the pregnancy, he instead took this visit as an opportunity to preach his political and religious beliefs to anyone who would listen.

"While we're waiting, can we maybe take this time to plan?" I softly asked him.

"Brianna, we don't even know what the fuck is going on… what do you POSSIBLY want to plan for?" he snickered.

"We can have an option A, B, and C based on what's going on, no?" I responded.

"You're stressing ME the fuck out," he said. *"And we're not even together."*

"That's what I wanted to talk about," I commented. *"If these symptoms are normal and the baby is fine, what do we do? Do you want to maybe get counseling and try and sort through these things?"*

"I don't believe in that," he sternly said. *"It's a waste of time."*

"Okay, well then what do you want to do, Hunter?" I said as I tightly squeezed my stomach to alleviate the pressure shooting across the lower half of my body.

"I want to not FUCKING talk about this right now and just figure out why you're bleeding," he said as he raised his voice. After five hours of no real answers or results, Hunter then insisted that he had to "leave to go to work."

He leaves you while you're pregnant with his child and experiencing complications.

RATIONALIZING THE RED FLAG: *"We're just entirely too toxic and he needs to separate for his own mental health. Hopefully, he'll come back around..."*

WHAT I SHOULD'VE DONE: Opened up to my loved ones about the circumstance that I was dealing with, as opposed to hiding this from everyone and hoping that I alone (with a not-so-good "partner") would prevail.

I FORGIVE MYSELF FOR: Trying to manage this situation alone... and for even getting myself here in the first place.

IF IT HAPPENS AGAIN: It won't.

SELF-LOVE LESSON: I can't play with fire. Though it initially may feel exhilarating and thrill-seeking to entertain a "flame" of a man, I must realize that I am not skilled enough to extinguish on command, let alone know how to even properly heal any burn wounds.

He left moments before I had to get a RhoGAM shot plowed directly into my left ass cheek, several more vials of blood sucked from my veins, and a long, plump vaginal ultrasound shoved up my blood-soaked pelvic area via probing. After he exited the hospital, these all-consuming feelings of neglect spiraled me into a full-blown panic attack. The sound of my tears deafened me until it was broken by the male nurse who barged into my room and sincerely questioned, *"Miss, what's going on? Are you okay?"*

"I'm really not," I wept. *"I'm spiraling, and I feel alone right now. I don't feel like I have the willpower to keep going."*

"I know we're still waiting for several lab results to come back, but I couldn't help but overhear some of your conversations," he lightly stated. *"Stress is really bad for a baby… and you… I'd advise you to try your best to curb it so that it doesn't further negatively impact your pregnancy or your mental health."*

"I can't!" I said. *"I'm trying, but he's making it so difficult,"* I added as my head fell into my hands and I sobbed.

"I know that you can do this," he comforted as he rubbed my shoulder.

The long-awaited lab results basically were inconclusive. According to the doctor, we didn't have any baseline hCG hormone levels to compare to in order to determine whether or not I was potentially miscarrying—though the symptoms seemed indicative of this outcome.

"I can most certainly rule out an ectopic pregnancy, though, based on the ultrasound," the doctor added, *"which is really good."*

"So now what?" I exhaustingly questioned after now having been stuck in the emergency room for nine hours.

"Again, this could be a miscarriage, or it could just be your body reacting to this change overall," the doctor stated. *"I advise that you call your OB/GYN and schedule routine blood work to monitor your hCG levels and determine the next steps from there."*

For the next few weeks, due to visitor restrictions, I had to chauffeur myself to my OB/GYN's office twice a week to have blood drawn. Initially, my hCG levels increased from my baseline hospital-levels of 306 to 477 in a matter of one week, which would typically be a positive sign. However, according to my doctor, the levels weren't rising at a normal rate. *"At this point, the levels should be almost doubling this early on in the pregnancy, which concerns me,"* she said.

Dealing with the emotions of an unexpected pregnancy with an absent partner spiraled me into a depression that I can't even put into words. I was mentally, physically, and emotionally teetering on a very fine line. As I remained in a state of confusion and denial, I started to consider an abortion as an option after spending countless hours crying. While still seeking care from my OB/GYN, I booked an online consultation at a Planned Parenthood clinic the following week.

"How are you going to make this decision without me?" he yelled as he finally called me in response to my text. *"And that's a fucking SIN!"*

"I've been ASKING for you and your help for WEEKS, Hunter!" I cried. *"It's not right to feel these fucking emotions and pains and have the partner who helped to create this not be by my side."*

"I'm fucking busy, Brianna!" he rebutted.

"And I'm FUCKING PREGNANT with YOUR child, Hunter!" I reiterated. *"What I envisioned to be this beautiful, invigorating journey where my partner is showering both me and our baby in love and affirmations is so starkly different from what's currently my reality."*

"Stop being so goddamn dramatic," he dismissed.

"You have no idea how much this is killing me," I cried. *"Any potential outcome that I can possibly think of I know will more than likely pain me for the rest of my life, and it pisses me off that I've had to deliberate this all on my own."*

The conversation with Hunter somehow convinced me to cancel my appointment at the clinic and I instead continued to seek counsel from my OB/GYN with our regularly scheduled visits. The immediate next blood draw at her office showed a dip in my hCG levels down to 317, then to 87 two weeks later, and then to 82 after two more weeks. My levels reached 15 the immediate next week. Essentially, my doctor explained to me that these decreasing levels signified the gradual loss of my baby. When I didn't have the lab results as reminders, I also had the daily blood clots and stab-like cramps that electrified my body, too. I prayed that somehow one of those shocks would make its way up to my heart and just end it all.

During the course of those twelve weeks as the phlebotomist continued to prick me with a butterfly needle until my hCG levels reached zero (or pre-pregnancy), Hunter only dedicated two quarter-days to me—and the remainder of those days he would only text me to demand updates on the pregnancy.

"Is it done yet?" he coldly questioned me.

Despite my transparency, he was convinced that I was "withholding" information. In fact, Hunter even texted me insisting that I somehow convince my OB/GYN to allow him access to the visit.

"If you don't believe me, here's the number to the office," I angrily texted back.

"I spoke to your doctor, and she is allowing me to listen to all visits moving forward from a phone call," he messaged back later that day.

On the final visit with my OB/GYN that determined that my body had naturally finalized the miscarriage without the need for a D&C (a surgical procedure to remove any remaining contents of the uterus after a first-trimester miscarriage), Hunter heard me piercingly cry through the phone that I couldn't believe that I had "lost my first baby." I'm genuinely surprised that my OB/GYN didn't call an ambulance to drive me into some kind of monitored mental institution from the way that I reacted to the information.

As I walked out of the doctor's office on autopilot and talked with Hunter, he said, *"I am sorry for your loss."*

He lacks empathy.

RATIONALIZING THE RED FLAG: *"He's just as drained from this relationship as I am… he doesn't have the head or heart space to care anymore."*

WHAT I SHOULD'VE DONE: Realized a while ago that I was dealing with someone who had exhibited several of the traits that clinicians use to diagnose someone with Narcissistic Personality Disorder… and lack of empathy is one of those signs.

I FORGIVE MYSELF FOR: Believing that this individual at this time in his life was capable of love.

IF IT HAPPENS AGAIN: It won't. I will recognize a lack of empathy as a deal breaker of a red flag in the future.

SELF-LOVE LESSON: I will not shame and blame myself for the could've, would've, and should'ves of this relationship. By being anchored by these negative thoughts, I would never allow myself to forgive and heal from the traumatic experiences that I endured in tandem with this individual.

"It was our baby, Hunter," I reminded him. *"You just didn't have this baby growing in you, affecting you, and changing your life so I guess it didn't matter much."*

"Are you okay?" he insincerely questioned.

"No," I responded. *"I need you. I needed you."*

"I'm sorry, Bri, but I have another event today that I'm on my way to," he said.

"Of course you do," I said as I then hung up the phone. Later that day, Hunter posted multiple pictures of him posing in front of American flag-themed backdrops. Hunter didn't reach out to me for a few days after that conversation. And so, I sank into the threads of my silk

"I just hate that I don't love myself," I continued to repeat.

"I promise that continuing down this path won't help," she reinforced.

Although I had previously begged to somehow accompany my unborn child and join its hands in an afterlife, I realized that my wish did partially come true: once I finally blocked Hunter out of my life after months of recalibration through professional help, "no contact," the support of loved ones, and journaling, that "old" part of me—the weak, desperate, and vulnerable side—did, in fact, die, too. Though traumatic in the sense that I grieved that part of me for having voluntarily endured those tragic experiences, I simultaneously was able to celebrate my rebirth.

By breaking that connection and regaining my power, I gradually instilled value back into myself through my own affirmations. I repeatedly reminded myself of my beauty, value, and worth, while promising myself to never allow someone the opportunity to stall or hinder my evolution ever again. My growth wouldn't have been possible without an agonizing reflective process, either. By taking accountability for my contribution to our dangerous cycle, I ultimately set my resentment toward him free and practiced authentic forgiveness. Hunter and I were two highly damaged individuals who sought love from the other to fill our voids.

You know, state-of-mind in addition to timing is everything. Looking back, I could've replaced Hunter with the man of my dreams—whether that be a papi lumberjack, Adam Sandler, or Michael Myers—and I wouldn't have been in the proper mental state to have accepted that person's energy. Realistically, it probably would've crashed and burned, too. Now pair that with another "broken" individual, and all the two of you will do is exacerbate the other's insecurities, faults, and toxic trauma responses and eventually spiral into chaos.

By coming to these revelations, I truly believe that I'm in the beginning phase of my own metamorphosis. While I pray to one day dance free in the winds like that of a butterfly, I pray that Hunter, too, can glide toward his migratory path in self-betterment.

Looking Within at Personal RED FLAGS

- You no longer recognize yourself when you look in the mirror.

- You don't really know who you are, but you think that a partner will help you figure it out. (Spoiler alert: they more than likely won't.)

- You stay in toxic situations.

- You love the idea of someone... but you don't actually love (or even like) that person.

- You devote countless hours to creeping on social media.

- You've given up your power and lost your identity.

- You accept less than you know you deserve.

- You question your own truth.

- You don't speak up due to a fear or rejection or conflict.

- You allow someone to tell you to "shut up" and immaturely communicate with you. (Again, you have no boundaries.)

- You treat red flags like roses... you're happy to be handed anything (as a nod to Trista Mateer's poetry book, *Artemis Made Me Do It*).

REAL.

[ˈrē(ə)l]

ADJECTIVE

1. actually existing as a thing or occurring in fact; not imagined or supposed

2. (of a substance or thing) not imitation or artificial; genuine

REVELATIONS

[revəˈlāSH(ə)ns]

NOUN

1. the making known of something that was previously secret or unknown

2. the divine or supernatural disclosure to humans of something relating to human existence or the world

13

THE GEMS
I GAINED

While writing some, if not all, of these chapters, I felt suffocated reflecting on the pain and trauma that I've experienced over the course of my life. I suppressed most of these memories by shoving them into a highly secured vault in the back of my mind. For the purposes of writing this book, though, I reluctantly knew that I had to pay it a visit. Reliving each and every story at once, over and over again, as I wrote, read, edited, and then rewrote the chapters almost broke me. I nearly flew the white flag at my publisher as I told her that I physically couldn't handle the effects that these pages were having on my body.

"Brianna, I encourage you to really, really take your time with this book," my publisher said.

"But I want this over!" I cried over Zoom. *"I don't have the strength in me to continue."*

"You don't need to dive this deeply this quickly," my editor warned. *"Just like a scuba diver who needs to avoid the bends by ascending or*

descending too rapidly, you need to slowly sink into these higher-pressure levels—and then every once in a while, you need to come up to the surface for air."

"*Everything feels so deep, though,*" I shared as I wiped my tears. "*I don't know how to maneuver these waters.*"

"*You're not giving yourself enough credit,*" my publisher added. "*Look at what you've been through… I promise you, you can do this.*"

Through constant pep talks with my publishing team, therapist, and loved ones, I thankfully learned how to better ground myself. I realized in an odd sense, that through the completion of this book, I could literally and figuratively "close the chapters" on all of those experiences and finally heal past them. That was the biggest motivating factor.

Every once in a while, though, I would still battle these feelings of: "*Why me? Why did I have to go through all of this? What is wrong with me?*"

Through writing, the common thread that wove itself in between all of these chapters was that I didn't love myself at my core. To some, I shockingly exude a false sense of confidence, but deep down I know that there is a battered woman who feels abused on too many levels. These men and my actions in choosing these men, therefore, were reflections of the love that I lacked in myself. I didn't respect myself enough to know what I shouldn't have endured, to know when something didn't feel "right," to truly trust myself, and—most importantly—to leave a situation that more than likely would be harmful. Instead, desperate to fill the voids that I actually needed to fill myself, I stayed with whichever person I happened to be with at the time.

These toxic situations multiplied like bacterial colonies within a Petri dish of negative self-talk that I observed not just under a microscope, but in real-time.

"*You deserved that pain,*" I'd yell at myself.

"*You'll never find love,*" I'd cry.

"*It's because you're ugly and fat,*" I'd wickedly say to my reflection.

"You may as well stay with him because you'll never find anyone that actually wants to be with you," I'd torment myself.

Over time, it didn't phase me when others would regurgitate the same negative comments back to me. How could I implement boundaries with others if I didn't even have them with myself? I couldn't—it felt almost hypocritical. I looked toward whichever masculine figure was in my life at the time to save me from my own downward plunge. One day, though, it hit me: if Rose couldn't protect Jack in the *Titanic*, I, too, needed to shake this thought that a "lover" would save me from drowning (from my thoughts). In the same regard, I also couldn't selfishly expect a person to stay attached to me out of my own abandonment issues while the person slowly deteriorated from whatever elements may have been dragging him down. I hoped to actually act on this enlightened thought.

In actuality, I remained in a terribly vicious cycle of fleeing one toxic situation, packing up that heavy baggage, hopping on the chaos train, and jumping off to unload at the next painful pit stop for quite some time. When I then entered that new terrible environment, most of the time I stayed out of fear of loneliness. Once I acknowledged that there were plenty of nights where I'd physically fall asleep next to my new energy-sucking vampire and emotionally feel miles apart, I amassed a new definition of loneliness. This prompted me to release myself from my own willful shackles.

I had the control to break this "prophecy" of sorts that I had to live a similar lifestyle of dysfunction that has trickled down my family's lineage. (And let's face it: we are all outcomes of this domino effect in one way or another.) I do say that in the most respectful of ways, though, especially to my mom.

My mom has endured more traumatic and heartbreaking scenarios than I could have ever possibly imagined, and yet she has found the strength to overcome. Although it is not my right to disclose more of her personal situations and invade her privacy (whereas I can mask the identities of others in this book), I understand the experiences that have molded and influenced many of her behaviors and decisions. Looking at my grandmother and grandfather's childhoods, too, I can identify the reasoning behind their own behaviors that inadvertently affected my mom. It is also through this same lens that we can visualize how sometimes an individual's decisions are guided merely by a survivalistic need to simply *live* day-by-day, and the consequences of such actions may be dealt with at a later time.

I opened my mind to this deeper understanding that we are all beautifully chaotic beings—and it is not our right to judge others, but to understand. Being that we humans are all works in progress (well, at least those of us who actually choose to do the work to grow and not remain stagnant), we must remain kind—even to the ones who have damaged us.

As for the individuals mentioned in this book, for some time I felt weighed down by the resentment, anger, and pain within my soul. I can wholeheartedly say, though, that I am in a mental space now where I have eradicated much of that negative energy. By releasing those intrusive feelings, I can now make room for positive feelings to seed and, over time, bloom into something even more beautiful. I do hope that each of these men can heal past the traumas and psychological barriers that caused them to act in the ways that they did so that they, too, can be better for themselves, first and foremost, and then for others.

Getting to this point has taken quite the effort through a partnership with my therapist. She guided me through this process of relinquishing control of not wanting to see these particular men be happy or successful in their own rights. Instead, I found an innate appreciation for escaping the situations that I was presented with—though not entirely unscathed—and gaining strength throughout the tumultuous process. Despite initially fearing the stigma that seems to surround therapy, I managed to pummel through those fictitious social constraints and readjust myself toward a path of betterment, enlightenment, and wholesomeness. Now open about my mental health, I have felt my overall power come back.

My therapist also helped me to tap into the essence of forgiveness of self and of others. As for myself, for years, I harbored shame as it pertained to many of my life decisions.

"I should have left him earlier," I'd sigh. *"I hate myself because I didn't."*

"Be kinder to yourself," she stated. *"Knowing what we know now, yes we can both agree that maybe you should've left earlier, but now you can own it, learn from it, mature from it, and know how to apply these principles to future decision-making."*

"Yeah, I guess you're right," I said.

"I know I am," she giggled.

"You'd think I'd know the red flags by now," I laughed back.

"I do believe that you know them," she replied, *"but you just didn't act on them."*

She was right: instead of stopping at the sight of a red flag, similar to that of a red stoplight, I blew through them and continued to do so because no officer caught me in the act. The only person who could patrol me through my own jurisdiction was me—except I was more fixated on obtaining instant gratification from a potential partner than adhering to the intricacies and time commitment of a true dating process. Impatient and weak, I had allowed anyone and everyone in a semi-romantic capacity the ability to hold complete access to me despite some of these indicators. Now, I recognize the red flags that I shouldn't *repeatedly* (or ever again) ignore, including:

- He asks for naughty pictures before he even really knows you.
- He doesn't go to the destination you agreed to.
- He doesn't want anyone to know about your connection.
- Your workplace is incredibly sexual in nature—and you contribute to the environment through your communication and actions.

- He drives while severely under the influence (which is also illegal).
- He tries to take advantage of you while you're under the influence (which is a crime).
- He calls his ex "crazy" without elaboration, clarification, or a deeper discussion.
- He doesn't care that other people are in the room when he starts sensually attacking you with his lips.
- He nonconsensually manipulates the situation to his benefit.
- He sadistically boasts about violence.
- He's not only encouraging excessive alcohol consumption, but he's filtering who he encourages said alcohol consumption to based on looks alone. (In other words, he's treating certain females differently based on their perceived levels of provocativity, "sluttiness," and overall sensuality.)
- He's flooded by comments from females on social media as they try to claim him while he, himself, appears single.
- He goes right to sex within minutes.
- He hands you a drink that he poured or mixed himself.
- He tries to and/or effectively fucks with you without a condom—and without even asking.
- He ghosts you.
- He tells you his red flag... and you blatantly ignore it.
- He goes from commitment-phobe to boyfriend within 24 hours.
- He turns his phone face down whenever he's with you.
- He disrespectfully speaks to his parents.
- He cheats on you.
- He doesn't accept your boundaries.

to survive and leave you in a state of deprivation. Once you nourish yourself by injecting love into your very being, you can then begin to branch out both literally and figuratively. At your core, you must believe that you are, in fact, worthy—and I promise you that you are.

Williams, Mrs. A, and Professor Simoes, thank you for all of your lessons. Sadly, some people may go through the years having not met an educator who transformed their mindsets—but I'm thankful enough to have met a handful within the same lifetime. You gifted me gems of language, editing, marketing, and higher-thinking that I graciously accepted and nurtured, and I wouldn't be the writer (or person) that I am today without your beautifully wise souls. Thank you for believing in me when, at times, I didn't believe in myself or my abilities in the scholastic setting.

There are so many other individuals who have played pivotal roles in my life like Little Neil, Lauren, Danny, Dan S., Coley, Biss, Mike O., Behnken, Michael D., Irwin, Bryan K., Tracy Morgan (I love and respect you more than I could ever explain), Wil, Ardie, KY, Jim (my Irish laddie), Jess K., Will, Joe, Karen, Cathy, Adam K., Kareem, Andy, Tyler, Olga, Bryant, Jon, Erica F., Scarlett, Danielle O., and more—but I'd probably write a book longer than this in trying to do each individual his or her proper justice. Believe me when I say that I am filled with gratitude, love, and abundance in knowing that I am surrounded by the most caring of souls. Thank you all for everything. Without you and the readers, *The Red Flags I've (Repeatedly) Ignored* would merely be a concept that forever lived in my mind.

It is my hope that this book can start each reader's inner (and sometimes highly avoidable) dialogue in recognizing who you are, what you deserve, and how to get there—while also appreciating the support system(s) at work. That, and of course I hope that Adam Sandler somehow stumbles upon this book, recognizes how much I admire him, and welcomes me to join him on future Happy Madison productions. (I feel like we'd all mesh beautifully if given the chance—although I can't promise I won't overdo it on the constant quoting of *Billy Madison* lines.)

xo Bri

BRIANNA MCCABE

 New Jersey

 Author, professor, and marketer

 October 6 #libragang

 MBA and BA from Monmouth University

 @thebriannamccabe